Political Performance:
A Twelve-Nation Study

TED ROBERT GURR
Department of Political Science
NORTHWESTERN UNIVERSITY

MURIEL McCLELLAND
Center of International Studies
PRINCETON UNIVERSITY

(S) SAGE PUBLICATIONS / **Beverly Hills**   **London**

For information address:

SAGE PUBLICATIONS, INC.
275 South Beverly Drive
Beverly Hills, California 90212

SAGE PUBLICATIONS, INC.
St George's House / 44 Hatton Garden
London E C 1

International Standard Book Number 0-8039-0161-5

Library of Congress Catalog Card No. 72-167877

FIRST PRINTING

CONTENTS

Introduction 5

THE DURABILITY OF POLITIES: INDICES AND
    COMPARISONS 10

Comparisons 17

CIVIL ORDER: INDICES AND COMPARISONS 17

LEGITIMACY 30

DECISIONAL EFFICACY: INDICES AND COMPARISONS 48

CROSS-POLITY COMPARISONS OF PERFORMANCE 69

A Concluding Comment 85

NOTES 85

REFERENCES 86

LIST OF TABLES AND FIGURES

Figure 1	The Durability of Polities, in Decades	15
Table 1	Survival Probabilities for Polities by Attained Age, from 30 Historical and Contemporary Cases	16
Table 2	Polity Durability	18
Table 3	Magnitudes of Civil Strife, ca. 1927-1936	27
Table 4	Magnitudes of Civil Strife, ca. 1957-1966	27
Table 5	Cross-Time Comparisons of Magnitudes of Strife	29
Table 6	Comparisons of Forms of Strife for all Polities	29
Table 7	Reliability and Validity of 1957-1966 Strife Measures	31
Table 8	List of Illegitimacy Manifestations	35
Table 9	Magnitude of Illegitimacy, ca. 1927-1936	40
Table 10	Magnitude of Illegitimacy, ca. 1957-1966	41
Table 11	Cross-Time Comparisons of Magnitudes of Illegitimacy, by Object and Characteristic	47
Table 12	Comparison of Aspects of Illegitimacy for all Polities	48
Table 13	Comparisons of Magnitudes of Strife and Illegitimacy, 21 Polities	49
Table 14	Efficacy of Budget Formation, ca. 1927-1936	54
Table 15	Efficacy of Budget Formation, ca. 1957-1966	55
Figure 2	Process of Authority Maintenance	56
Table 16	Decisional Efficacy: Maintenance of Authority, ca. 1927-1936	62
Table 17	Decisional Efficacy: Maintenance of Authority, ca. 1957-1966	64
Table 18	Summary Efficacy Scores, ca. 1927-1936	68
Table 19	Cross-Time Comparisons of Selected Measures of Decisional Efficacy	69
Table 20	Comparisons of Measures of Budgetary Efficacy, all Polities	70
Table 21	Comparisons of Measures of Authority Maintenance, all Polities	70
Table 22	Comparisons of Summary Measures of Efficacy, all Polities	70
Table 23	Summary Measures of Performance in Standard Scores	72
Table 24	Comparisons of Summary Performance Measures with Durability, by Decade and for all Polities	73
Figure 3	Profiles of Polity Performance, ca. 1927-1936	74
Figure 4	Profiles of Polity Performance, ca. 1957-1966	75
Table 25	Average Performance Scores for Democratic and Authoritarian Polities, all Cases	76
Table 26	Multiple Regression Estimates of Polity Durability	77
Table 27	Partial Correlations Among Performance Variables	78
Figure 5	Hypothetical Causal Model Among Performance Dimensions	79
Figure 6	Empirical Causal Model Among Performance Dimensions, Showing Dominant Relationships Only	79

Political Performance:
A Twelve-Nation Study

TED ROBERT GURR
Northwestern University

MURIEL McCLELLAND
Princeton University

INTRODUCTION

The conceptual groundwork for research reported here has been fully laid down in Eckstein (1971). Our ultimate object is to evaluate theories about the general determinants of the performance of polities. This requires two prior tasks: specification of what is meant by political performance generally; the development of operational measures to determine how well or badly particular polities have in fact performed at any particular time. Eckstein maintains there are at least four crucial dimensions of political performance, dimensions on which polities must perform well to some degree if they are to attain any special goals (other than their own dissolution). Our labels for these all-but-axiomatic dimensions are *durability, civil order, legitimacy,* and *decisional efficacy*.

This paper offers three rather different kinds of contributions to the study of performance. The first is workable operational procedures for measuring our four dimensions of performance. Much of the academic debate about performance has centered on questions of how best to conceptualize its nature and causes, a debate that has not encouraged efforts at operational assessment. The procedures outlined in the first four major sections are

AUTHORS' NOTE: *This is a report on empirical work carried out in the Workshop in Comparative Politics at Princeton University, which is directed by Harry Eckstein and this paper's senior author. The report deals with our efforts to operationalize a conceptualization of political performance that is the subject of Harry Eckstein's companion paper on "The Evaluation of Political Performance: Problems and Dimensions" (Sage Professional Papers 01-017, 1971). A number of individuals other than* operational "solutions" some may find sufficient, and which should stimulate proponents of other conceptual viewpoints to develop their own.

One proof of an operational method rests with the results of its application to real cases. Our second contribution is to report the results of a thorough application of our procedures to twelve countries, ten of them in two eras of their histories. The quantitative results are generally consistent with conventional, ideographic evaluations of these countries' performance, and are suitable for relatively more precise comparisons. Scores for each country on each aspect of the four dimensions are presented in the above-mentioned sections. The indicators are accompanied by a sample of narrative summaries of the phenomena they represent.[1]

The last and in some ways most intriguing contribution of the study arises from the comparisons reported in the last section. We propose and evaluate a probabilistic, causal model of the relations among the performance indicators, making both synchronic and diachronic comparisons of the data. The results suggest that a forecasting model of a polity's durability can be devised. Levels of efficacy, legitimacy, and civil order all appear to have an interacting, time-dependent relationship with a polity's longevity. The empirical base for the causal model assessed here is much too limited to provide any basis for forecasts, certainly not beyond the limits of the twelve countries studied. The results do not suggest that precise, "point" predictions can be made about polity life-spans. But if the empirical base were to be considerably expanded, we should be able to attain means for making probability forecasts with modest accuracy.

An Approach to Operationalization

From the outset, we had in mind certain criteria to be satisfied by any operational measures of performance. Satisfactory measures should be

Professor Eckstein and the coauthors were instrumental to the research. We owe a special debt to James Testa and Mary Fosler, who patiently and meticulously collected great quantities of information and helped us interpret and code it. Other data were gathered by Thomas Reepmeyer. Erika Gurr coded much of the data and helped in its analysis. A number of Princeton graduate students whose interests paralleled ours provided criticisms of our procedures and evaluation of their results; most are listed in note 2 (at the end of this paper). Gurston Dacks and Harry Eckstein provided helpful critiques of the manuscript as a whole. This and other of our research reports thus owe much to assistance and collaboration not reflected in the authorship credits of a particular paper.

This project was initially supported by Princeton University and the Advanced Research Projects Agency, Department of Defense; more recently it has been supported by the National Science Foundation. Much of this report was written during 1970, while the senior author was the recipient of a Ford Foundation Faculty Fellowship. This varied support does not imply that any sponsor has approved this paper, nor that the authors necessarily support operating policies of the granting agencies. A summary of this paper was presented at the Annual Meeting of the International Studies Association, Section on Polimetrics, March 17-20, 1971, at San Juan, Puerto Rico.

applicable to all kinds of polities, irrespective of their forms and the particular goals they might seek. Moreover, the measures ought not be implicitly biased to give higher scores to, say, multi-party democracies than one-party socialist regimes, or vice versa. Nor ought they specially favor polities that pursue such policies as rapid economic growth over those that promote egalitarian poverty, for example, or traditional community virtue. The study does have normative implications: civil order, legitimacy, and efficient decision-making are commonly judged "good things," and our measures may facilitate normative evaluations based on the extent of such conditions. We have especially tried to avoid unexamined premises with normative connotations, such as the assumption that polities with formal political competition are inherently more legitimate than one-party or no-party polities.

We attempted to operationalize the dimensions as fully as possible to reduce the "slippage," as it is sometimes called, between concept and indicator. Similarly, we wanted to devise measures with a fair degree of prima facie validity, and discarded many possible scales and some bodies of data because they seemed inappropriate or irrelevant. Operational procedures reported here have sufficient precision that the reliability of the measures should be determinable as well. Some initial reassessments of reliability and validity are reported.

As a practical criterion, the minimal information required to assess a polity's performance should be available for a substantial number of polities for a considerable time-span. There is not much empirical merit in comparative measures which require data obtainable for only a handful of polities, however elegant their conceptualization and precise their scales. We revised and discarded a number of scales on these grounds.

With these criteria in mind, we did not expect to operationalize the performance dimensions with single indices or conventional aggregate statistics. Most of the major concepts of political science, like power, legitimacy, authority, and conflict cannot be simply indexed. Three responses to these various measurement difficulties prevail in comparative studies. They are: to eschew measurement and rely largely on verbal description and summary judgments; to work from available statistical data, denoting concepts with precise, but questionably relevant, indices; to make general judgments based on superficial information forced onto scales that afford few and often imprecise distinctions. This study took a fourth course, which has four distinctive though not novel characteristics:

- the primary sources are narrative historical materials and commentaries, from which information relevant to the dimensions and concepts is culled;
- the information so collected provides the basis for coding a set of interval and ordinal scales, each of the latter usually using five or six categories that are rather precisely illustrated;

    —each dimension is represented by a set of measures, both to maximize the amount of information taken into account in summary measures and to permit comparisons among its aspects;

    —judgmental scales are treated as interval scales for the purpose of combining and statistically comparing them.

Each of these features of our approach to operationalization has disadvantages that offset some of its advantages. The use of historical materials makes it possible to take account of information in a richness and detail not ordinarily used or usable in conventional aggregate-data studies, but requires a very substantial investment of research time; more than three man-years were required to collect and evaluate the information for the countries and variables included in this study. The quantification of historical materials makes it possible to index and compare concepts which have been previously operationalized poorly or not at all, but the use of judgmental scales raises questions about the validity of the indicators and the reliability of coders that we can only begin to answer. The use of multiple measures of each variable helps allay the criticism that single measures of complex conditions are useless because they ignore too much important variation, but our combination of these multiple measures into summary ones raises the same criticism transformed by one turn of the screw: the conditions whose measures are being combined may seem incommensurable. Finally, the treatment of judgmental data as though they were zero-order interval data, susceptible to all arithmetical and statistical manipulations, will offend methodological purists in spite of the now-conventional argument that many important comparisons cannot otherwise be made.

From our point of view, two advantages should outweigh all these disadvantages: narrative historical materials are further opened up to quantitative comparisons by these techniques, and concepts which have obdurately resisted quantitative analysis for want of sufficient data are now more susceptible to precise description and theoretical explanation. The adequacy of the data generated in this and future studies, and the results of their analysis, should help arbitrate questions about the adequacy of the procedures used to gather them. We make two other claims for our data as well. They go beyond the arbitrary judgments about what is high performance that characterize some discussions of the subject, however informed those judgments may be. And neither the dimensions nor the data that operationalize them have been preselected to support theories or hunches about why performance should be high or low in general or in particular cases.

The primary data sources for all dimensions except durability were the *New York Times* and its annual indexes, supplemented for every country by historical sources. We hold no brief for the *Times* as a perfect historical source, but for comparative studies seeking moderate rather than exquisite detail, it is not only adequate for most larger countries—after the 1920s, at least—but indispensable. It has one unquestionable advantage over mono-graphic secondary sources: whereas monographs are selective according to the purposes of their authors, which seldom coincide with ours, the *Times* attempts with partial success to provide a diurnal record of significant events. The *Times* must be used in conjunction with secondary studies and commentaries, of course, always in order to ascertain the general context of events, often to obtain some perspective on their ramifications, and where possible to supplement the detail often lacking in summary news reporting. The only better strategy would be to rely on a combination of monographic literature and the press of the countries studied. The detail would unquestionably be greater, but the task of sifting and summarizing it would increase hugely. One partial alternative is to have narrative summaries of events and coding judgments reviewed by country experts; this has been done with much of the narrative materials prepared in connection with this paper. It is to be hoped that some future studies of these dimensions will rely on the foreign press and make greater use of panels of experts to answer better the questions of source reliability.

Countries and Eras Studied

Twelve countries are included in this study: Canada, Colombia, France, Germany/West Germany, Italy, Mexico, the Netherlands, the Philippines, Spain, Sweden, Tunisia, and Yugoslavia. Eleven are represented by data on all four dimensions, Tunisia on the three for which information was available. The selection of these countries was expedient rather than systematic: they are the countries chosen for fieldwork by graduate students in our seminars at Princeton University, who made their choices on the bases of individual interest and accessibility.[2] The countries are not a representative sample in the conventional sense, but they are representative of several important dimensions of variation. Western and non-Western countries are included. Their polities include both stable and unstable, pluralistic and authoritarian regimes. Most important for our theoretical concerns, they include a number of polities that experienced major, sometimes revolutionary collapses or transformations before or after the eras we studied. Few and tentative statistical generalizations from the results of our analyses are warranted, but the synchronic and diachronic comparisons within the set are of much substantive and theoretical interest.

A decade was initially selected as an optimum time-span for assessing each performance dimension, except durability, because most are subject to short-term fluctuations that a general evaluation ought to average out. We also wished to evaluate long-term trends in performance, so for the more long-lived countries in the sample—all except the Philippines and Tunisia—we collected data on two decades separated by a substantial time-lag. We first collected data for identical periods for all countries, 1927-1936 and 1957-1966. The more recent decade was chosen because it immediately preceded the beginning of our research and students' fieldwork. The earlier decade of reference had the advantage that the immediate effects of World War I on European governments had passed by 1927, while the dislocations of World War II antedated 1936. The choice of the late 1920s and early 1930s also allowed us to observe how various polities responded to the enormous impact of the Great Depression. Several crumbled under that impact, most staggered, but a few dealt promptly and effectively with its stresses. Our two decades of reference included parts of the lifespans of two or more polities in several countries. Germany I included parts of both the Weimar Republic and the Nazi state, for example, while 1957-1966 in France saw the last year of the Fourth Republic and the first years of the Fifth. Consequently we changed some periods of reference. Germany in the early period is represented in this paper by data for the last ten years of the Weimar Republic, 1923-1932, and France II is represented by data for the first ten years of the Fifth Republic. Other such adjustments are identified in the first major section, below. The consequent lack of precise synchronization detracts from the panel design of the study, but is more than compensated for by the conceptual appropriateness of the results and comparisons.

THE DURABILITY OF POLITIES: INDICES AND COMPARISONS

Durability refers to the persistence or longevity of a polity. Our interest in the dimension is qualified by the normative recognition that survival is not an intrinsic good. There is some merit in a polity's longevity if it substitutes for misery and violence. But longevity can also coexist with and sometimes depend upon misery and repression, as in South Africa, Albania since 1945, and Haiti from 1957 to 1971. We suspect, though, that these are unusual—i.e., deviant—cases and that durability generally is a function of polities' skill at protecting and creating the conditions and goods valued by their citizens. Some decisional efficacy is needed to accomplish such tasks; to accomplish them is likely in turn to enhance legitimacy and civil order. In other words, we differ slightly from Eckstein's view of durability as one of four simultaneous, interacting dimensions of performance (1971: 21-32). We think of it as principally a consequence of high performance on the other three dimensions considered in this study. Our conceptualization does not exclude feedback effects of durability on other performance dimensions. A polity's legitimacy in particular is likely to be enhanced by its longevity. But generally we think that some degree of efficacy, civil order, and legitimacy is precursor of, and requisite for, durable polities. The converse does not seem to us likely in any but the rarest circumstances. Some simple causal analyses are done in the section beginning on page 69 as a preliminary test of this hypothesis.

Operational Distinctions

Durability is not so simple a concept as it seems, nor is it entirely easy to operationalize. One subsidiary definition is needed to clear away a possible source of confusion: by "polity" we mean the basic political arrangements by which national political communities govern their affairs, not the political communities themselves. In common usage, a polity is said to endure if it persists for a long time without disruptive changes. A common qualification is that a system be regarded as durable if it has undergone fundamental change which occurred gradually. The English polity, for example, has changed fundamentally since the late seventeenth century, but in a series of gradual increases in parliamentary authority vis-à-vis the monarchy, reforms in suffrage and representation, and extension of governmental regulation and control. This suggests three specific, operational questions: what aspects of a polity must change before we question its durability, how much, and how quickly?

Our operational definition of durability is based on the length of time a polity endures without abrupt, major change in the pattern of authority relations among its basic elements. The basic elements of a polity are its structures of rule-making and rule-application, and its citizens or subjects. In one-party and one-party-dominant states, the party also is a basic element. In federal systems, the nation and, collectively, the regional governments are basic elements. Change is _abrupt_ if the shift from one pattern to another occurs in ten years or less; it is _major_ if the relative power or status of one or more of the basic elements is in practice fundamentally changed vis-à-vis the others. A working list of such fundamental changes, applicable to Western and most non-Western systems, follows:

   I. Change from any of these patterns of executive-legislative relationships to another: executive-legislative parity; monarch-dominant; dictator- or _junta_-dominant; president-dominant; cabinet-dominant; legislature-dominant; one-party dominant
  II. Change from either of these forms of state organization to the other: federal system; centralized system
 III. Changes among any of the following patterns of government-citizen relations:
    (1) competitive elections; noncompetitive elections
    (2) elections for most or all national offices; elections for few or no national offices
    (3) change in suffrage affecting more than 50% of the adult male population
 IV. Changes from any of these scopes of governmental authority to another:

minimal; governmental authority is limited largely to such core functions as maintenance of security and administration of justice, and including the "predatory state," in which the elite exploits the system primarily for its own benefit
segmental; the government exercises direct control over substantial sectors of socioeconomic activity, but major sectors maintain substantial autonomy
comprehensive; the government exercises control over most or all sectors of socioeconomic activity.

Such changes are not necessarily abrupt, as noted above. The United States has since its founding changed from executive-legislative parity to a president-dominant system (in practice, in some spheres of action) and from minimal to segmental scopes of authority, but both these changes have been gradual. When they are abrupt, several such changes are likely to occur more or less simultaneously. The Mexican Revolution, 1911-1917, accomplished a change from what was in practice a dictatorial pattern to a president-dominant pattern, and a change from minimal to segmental governmental control. The Russian Revolution resulted in a change from monarchy to a one-party state, from a unitary to a nominally-federal system, from competitive to noncompetitive elections, and from segmental to comprehensive governmental control. Examples of single but nonetheless fundamental changes from countries included in this study are the institutionalization of the Mexican Revolution in a dominant party, 1929-1934 (president-dominant to one-party dominant) and the establishment of the French Fifth Republic, 1958-1962 (legislature-dominant to president-dominant).

Another point to be made is that we regard a change in the formal powers of an executive, legislature, or the government as whole, as a *major* change only if accompanied by substantial change in practice. In Yugoslavia in 1931, for example, King Alexander proclaimed the end of his dictatorship and introduced a new constitution, but in fact retained personal rule until his assassination three years later. Cabinet-dominant government was not fully reestablished until 1939, and then was accompanied by a shift from a unitary to a federal system. The entire sequence of changes from 1931 to 1939 constitutes an abrupt change in power relationships. Moreover, changes in practice are not necessarily codified by formal, constitutional changes. In Colombia in 1953, General Rojas Pinilla seized power in a coup and ruled for four years as a dictator, but maintained a facade of legality under the previous constitution. These qualifications should make it emphatically clear that the durability of a polity can be adequately judged only with substantial information on the political history of the system.

One other qualification is that political changes imposed by external authority, for example by an occupying or colonial power, are not "abrupt changes" in this study. Such changes are obviously consequential, but they are not commonly determined or substantially affected by the other

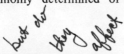

dimensions of performance in our scheme. The same kind of limitation applies to the formation of new nations—e.g., by union of adjacent territories or by a colony's attainment of autonomy. We use such transitions to mark the birth of political communities and polities, not as "abrupt changes" in the political arrangements of existing nations.

The simplest way of determining the durability of specific polities is to identify their last abrupt, major change and measure it against a standard. Lipset uses a temporally fixed standard to obtain a dichotomous measure: if the last change occurred before World War I, a polity is stable, otherwise it is unstable (Lipset, 1960: 30). Flanigan and Fogelman (1968) use a moving base point: in each of a number of historical eras they code democratic polities as "successful" if they have survived two decades without major change. One drawback to such procedures is that they dichotomize what is conceptually a continuous variable: there are degrees of longevity we wish to take into account. The simplest *continuous* measure is the number of years a polity endures between the abrupt, major changes that mark its establishment and termination. A limitation of this procedure is that it exaggerates the difference between an on-going polity like the Canadian, without abrupt change since the Dominion was established in 1867, and the United States, without abrupt polity change since 1789. Persistence of a pattern for 103 years is conceptually little less consequential than persistence of another for 181 years, yet a score based on years alone indicates that the American polity is 78% "more durable" than the Canadian. This suggests that some kind of rescaling be used for data on durability, giving relatively more weight to differences between survival spans of, say, 20 and 40 years, than between 60 and 80.

Polity Life Spans and Durability

It was neither desirable nor necessary to devise abstract measures of polity durability without empirical material. Consequently we gathered basic data on the incidence and nature of major polity changes in each of this study's twelve countries, for the period 1840 to 1970 inclusive. This information was collected from many historical sources, with substantial reliance on William Langer's *Encyclopedia of World History* (1968), especially for the nineteenth century. Polity changes briefly imposed by an occupying foreign power, such as Japan in the Philippines and Germany and Italy in Yugoslavia during World War II, were not scored as changes. Postwar reversion to the prewar pattern, as in the Netherlands and the Philippines, was regarded as continuity of the polity. Postwar resort to a new pattern, as in Yugoslavia, was treated as a major, abrupt change.

We distinguish the origins of 39 distinct polities in these twelve countries, only one of which—Sweden—has had the same polity throughout the

131-year period covered. Canada, however, has had a single polity lasting from 1867 to the present. Colombia is typical of the seven countries that have had multiple polities. The first (in our data) was established in the 1850s and lasted to the 1880s, the second endured until 1953, the third was a four-year dictatorship, and a fourth began in 1958 and has continued through 1970. We had no serious problems of identification for Colombia or other countries: successive polities were in most instances clearly distinguishable, sometimes separated by transition periods of several years. In no instance did we find an apparent transition period of more than ten years, which tends to support the operational decision to define "abrupt" changes as those occurring in ten years or less. We arbitrarily dated the births and deaths of polities to the end of transitional periods and counted their life spans to the nearest decade.[3] The first Colombian polity, for example, lasted from ca. 1863 to ca. 1885 = 22 years = 2 decades. The results are summarized in the bar graph in Figure 1, which distinguishes between the 27 historical polities whose full life spans can be assessed, and the 12 continuing, contemporary polities.

The brevity of polity life is striking: the average life span, including the continuing polities, is about 29 years, little more than one human generation. Among the 27 historical polities, 21 were terminated within less than one generation of their establishment. The six longer-lived ones include three that were terminated under the impact of World Wars I or II (Imperial Germany, pre-Fascist Italy, and the French Third Republic); a fourth ended during an internal war (Colombia, 1953). On the other hand, the Spanish constitutional monarchy was terminated in 1923 after nearly 50 years, with only a slight push by General Primo de Rivera. In our limited data, then, the survival of a polity beyond one generation suggests that it probably but not certainly will survive later crises.

The distributions of both historical and continuing polities in Figure 1 provide a basis for rescaling that gives greater weight to a polity's survival during its early years. The following eight-point scale is used for some subsequent scoring:

Polity Duration in Years	0-5	6-10	11-15	16-25	26-40	41-55	56-75	76+
Durability Score	0	1	2	3	4	5	6	7

Eckstein (1971: 26) has suggested on abstract grounds that no distinctions be made among polities that survive for less than a half-generation, or 10-15 years. Among our historical polities, however, we find that fully 15 were terminated before their sixteenth year, six of them during their first five years; five more between their sixth and tenth years. This high incidence of "infant mortality" suggests the operational usefulness of finer distinctions at the lower end of the durability scale.

One drawback of this scale, and any such measure, is its inapplicability to those continuing polities that are less than 76 years old. The West German Federal Republic, for example, was 21 years old in 1970; to score its durability "3" is to group it with polities that survived no more than 25 years. We used the empirical data on historical polities to determine survival probabilities for polities of a given age, and applied these to the younger continuing polities. The probabilities are shown in Table 1; note that we included in the empirical base the three continuing polities aged 76+ in 1970. Based on these data, the "life expectancy" of the West German Federal Republic in 1970 can be estimated by interpolation as about 50 years: of the polities that had previously survived 21 years, half were terminated by age 50 or so. The scores shown in Table 2 for nine young continuing polities in 1970 were determined by this procedure. The probabilities are of course based on a limited and unsystematic sample. More precise information for a variety of types of polities would provide more reliable probabilities. Note that this is a data-estimation technique, based on a kind of persistence prediction. Data on other dimensions of performance, when analyzed in the last major section with durability scores, provide a possible basis for contingency forecasts.

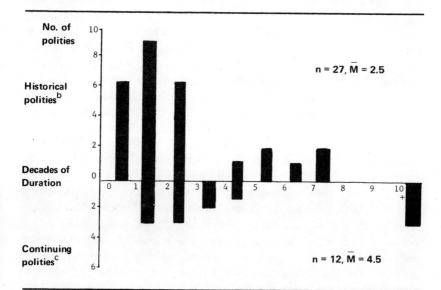

a. Data on polities from the 12 countries included in this study, from the mid-nineteenth century to 1970. See text.

b. Longevity of polities no longer in existence, i.e., the number of decades survived before termination.

c. Duration of the 12 polities as of January 1971, i.e., the number of decades thus far survived.

Figure 1: THE DURABILITY OF POLITIES, IN DECADES[a]

TABLE 1
SURVIVAL PROBABILITIES FOR POLITIES BY ATTAINED AGE
FROM 30 HISTORICAL AND CONTEMPORARY CASES[a]

	Probability of Survival to Age					Life Expectancy
Attained Age	5	15	25	55	75	(p=.5)[b]
0 years	.8	.5	.3	.2	.1	15 years
5 years		.6	.4	.3	.1	20 years
15 years			.6	.4	.2	40 years
30 years				.7	.3	65 years
55 years					.5	75 years

a. Including 27 historical cases from seven countries plus three continuing cases of long-lived polities (Canada, Netherlands, and Sweden).

b. By extrapolation; rounded.

Table 2 lists polity durability scores for two periods, one for the incumbent polity during the 1920s and 1930s, the second for the incumbent polity in the 1950s and 1960s. Since several polities were terminated during our decades of reference, 1927-1936 and 1957-1966, we adjusted scoring periods for other performance dimensions to coincide with their life spans. In the early period, we made the following adjustments. For Spain we include only the Republican period to the onset of the Civil War, 1932-1936 inclusive. For Yugoslavia we include the full span of its only prewar polity of any duration, the constitutional monarchy from 1921-1928. The German data are for the Weimar Republic, 1923-1932. Only two adjustments were needed for the second period: we coded France for the first decade of the Fifth Republic, 1959-1968, and Colombia for 1958-1967, which followed the restoration of two-party rule after a four-year dictatorial interlude.[4]

Two sets of durability scores are used, one a set of "raw scores" giving the life of each polity rounded to the nearest five years (long-lived polities = 100), the other the scaled scores discussed above. "Life expectancy" estimates are used for the younger continuing polities in the second period. A fifth set of "instability" scores also is included, indicating in raw and scaled scores the average life spans of historical polities in those ten countries for which there is substantial historical experience on which to draw. These scores index the historical ability of national political communities to create durable polities and provide an instructive contrast to the "life expectancies" shown for the younger continuing polities. In France, for example, the life expectancy of the Fifth Republic, based on its attained age alone, is 35 years, contrasted with the sixteen-year-average life span of the six preceding French polities. The same kind of difference characterizes the other continuing polities: all have current life expectancies substantially greater than suggested by their historical instability. A possible interpretation is that contemporary polities tend to be more durable than their predecessors. An alternative, technical interpretation is that the expectancies are overstated—by inclusion of the long-lived polities in the data base—and ought to be weighted by reference to historical instability in each country. Our data base for polities and countries would have to be substantially expanded to provide a basis for deciding between these interpretations.

There is another basis for questioning the reliability of some of the "life expectancy" estimates. In impressionistic comparison, the political immobilism of Spain under General Franco for 32 years inspires less confidence in its ultimate longevity than is inspired by the successful alternation of both chief executives and ruling party in the West German Federal Republic during its briefer, 21-year history. Two continuing polities in our sample have immobilistic regimes besides Spain: Tunisia and Yugoslavia. In an earlier stage of analysis, we adjusted their durability estimates downward, but not in the analyses reported here. The effects of immobilism on durability can best be determined by further empirical work.

COMPARISONS

The data in Table 2 provide a basis for a few simple comparisons. The average durability of polities in the countries studied increased from the early to the late period. The later durability data are mostly estimates of life expectancy, but the conjecture that life expectancy has increased is supported by the fact that all five of the short-lived polities of the first era—those of Mexico, Spain, Italy, Germany, and Yugoslavia—are now succeeded by polities that by 1970 had already outlasted their predecessors of the 1920s.

The durability of specific polities also can be compared with the long-run capacity of their political communities to produce stable polities. Durability in the first era, measured in years, correlates .86 with "instability"; the r for the second era is .87 ($n = 10$ in both comparisons). To put the matter plainly, historical instability is a rather good predictor of contemporary instability.

A technical comparison was made between the two alternative measures of durability, "years" and the 0-to-8 scale scores, by combining the 22 polities of both eras. The measures correlate almost perfectly, $r = .96$, as is to be expected. Skewness statistics, however, show that the "years" measure is considerably more normal in distribution than the scaled scores, and hence for this sample of polities is technically better suited for statistical comparisons.[5]

CIVIL ORDER: INDICES AND COMPARISONS

Civil order refers here to the absence of collective resorts to violence, and actions that are latently violent, to achieve private or public objectives. By

TABLE 2
POLITY DURABILITY

| Country | Basic Institutional Established | Polity Durability | | | | | | Instability | |
| | | First Period | | | Second Period | | | (Average Life Span of Historial Polities)[d] | |
		Life Span	Age[a]	Score	Life Span	Age[a]	Score	Age	Score
Sweden	14th century	1809-pres.	100+	7	1809-pres.	100+	7	100+(1)	7
Netherlands	1579	1848-pres.	100+	7	1848-pres.	100+	7	100+(1)	7
Canada	1867	1867-pres.	100+	7	1867-pres.	100+	7	100+(1)	7
Mexico	1824	ca. 1917-1934	15	3	ca. 1935-pres.	70[b]	6[b]	22 (4)	3
Spain	1812	1931-1939	10	1	1939-pres.	70[b]	6[b]	15 (6)	2
Philippines	1935	— —	—	—	1935-pres.[c]	65[b,c]	6[b]	—	—
Italy	1861	ca. 1922-1943	20	3	1947-pres.	55[b]	5[b]	42 (2)	5
Germany	1871	1919-1933	15	2	1949-pres.	50[b]	5[b]	24 (3)	3
Yugoslavia	1918	1921-1929	10	1	1950-pres.	50[b]	5[b]	7 (3)	1
Tunisia	1957	— —	—	—	1957-pres.	40[b]	4[b]	—	—
Colombia	1811	1886-1953	65	6	1958-pres.	35[b]	4[b]	24 (3)	3
France	1792	1879-1940	60	6	1958-pres.	35[b]	4[b]	16 (6)	3
Means			50	4.3		64	5.5	45.0	

a. Age of polity at termination, rounded to the nearest five years. Continuing polities of 100 years + are recorded as 100.

b. Life expectancies of continuing polities, derived from Table 1.

c. The wartime interregnum, 1942-1946, is excluded from the base used in estimating life expectancy.

d. For the period surveyed, including only polities established and terminated between ca. 1840 and 1970. Figures in parentheses are the number of such polities per country.

violence, we mean deliberate uses of force to physically injure or destroy, not some more general and less observable category of coercive actions or policies, and not institutional arrangements that demean or frustrate their members. "Collective" signifies our concern with group actions, as distinct from individual acts. "Latently violent" actions are those that as a class have a substantial probability of violence: examples are mass confrontations between citizens and police, and coups d'état at gunpoint, in both of which violence occurs or does not according to whether a rock is thrown or a trigger pulled. *Civil strife* is the term used here for both violent and latently violent actions and interactions.

It should be obvious that civil order signifies high performance from a statist point of view, not necessarily from others. As Eckstein (1971: 38) observes, "private groups often rightly think that civil disorder is to their advantage or that they have no alternative." However, we are concerned with the performance of the polity. Whoever its incumbents and whatever their objectives, high and enduring levels of strife are almost certainly dysfunctional, whether strife is used as an instrument of rule, of opposition, or of private conflict resolution. Another qualification, probably also obvious, is that complete civil order is not a requisite for high performance, and in fact is so unlikely among contemporary polities that its apparent occurrence is grounds for questioning the reliability of information. We might expect an otherwise ineffective polity to be relatively free of strife for some years because it lacked societal strains that tested the limited capacities of its elite. An otherwise effective polity may use or experience considerable violence for a brief period because of crises that cannot either be anticipated or immediately resolved. But neither is likely to be entirely orderly for any substantial time, and both are likely in the long run to have civil order or civil strife in proportion to their performance on other dimensions.

We can distinguish three kinds of civil strife events according to the kinds of groups involved: (1) private strife, engaging two private groups such as workers and employers, or religious factions; (2) public strife, engaging two official factions, for example in a purge or "palace revolution"; and (3) political strife, in which public and private groups oppose one another in such events as political riots, civil wars, and terroristic repression. Eckstein (1971: 38) distinguishes events in (3) between those in which public groups act against private ones, and those in which private groups act against public ones. The distinction is important for many legal and analytic purposes, but its operational application to summary sources involves us in many chicken-and-egg problems. Who starts a riot, the demonstrators who asemble before the National Palace or the militiamen who fire at them? Who began the French Revolution, the Court party or the National Assembly? The Parisians who mobbed the Bastille or the superannuated soldiers who chose to defend it? The forms of strife are much more reliably identified than their prime movers. As one result our operational procedures are based on the incidence and extent of the more visible forms of strife. The procedures described below require one initial qualification. Violence initiated by governments as a recurrent means of control, such as "reigns of terror" and the purging or suppression of whole classes and groups of citizens, are not included here. These are seldom discrete "events" but long-term policies. We use them in evaluating a polity's legitimacy (see the section beginning on p. 30, below) on grounds that they serve to identify groups—the victims—that reject intensely the legitimacy of the polity.

Operational Approaches

Civil order is indexed here using measures of the magnitude of various forms of strife in each polity; the higher a polity's strife scores, the farther it deviates from complete civil order. Characteristics of strife have been measured more often and in a greater variety of ways than almost any other aspect of performance, so initially we had to choose among many alternative approaches. The absolute numbers of various categories of events have been counted, for example by Rummel (1965) and Hudson (1970). Some specific measured characteristics of strife are man-days of participation (Tilly and Rule, 1965); deaths from group conflict (Rummel, 1965, and Russett, 1964); and social area, duration, and intensity of civil disturbances (Sorokin, 1937, and Gurr with Ruttenberg, 1967). Various composite measures, using these and other characteristics, have been devised as well, including measures of "magnitude" devised by Sorokin (1939) and Gurr (1968), and the Feierabends' (1966) "political instability" profiles.

We excluded absolute measures of strife in favor of proportional ones, which are more appropriate for most comparisons among nations. For example, if nations are of greatly different size, the significance of strife for their political systems is more accurately compared by examining the proportion of each country affected by demonstrations or rebellions than by comparing the absolute numbers of such events, even if those numbers could be determined with any reliability. Populations of the countries in the study vary widely, ranging in 1966 from Tunisia with 4.5 million to West Germany with 57.5 million. Several of the proportionality measures used elsewhere in the literature are conceptually appropriate but have operational limitations. The scaling procedures devised by the Feierabends (1966) require relatively precise counting and categorization of events. Scores calculated by these procedures are substantially affected by the adequacy of reporting in whatever sources are used: the better the sources the higher the scores. The procedures used by Gurr (1968) to determine "magnitude of strife" require more time-consuming collection of such data as numbers of people involved and casualties, for a gain in precision that did not seem worthwhile for purposes of general assessment of performance. The procedures used here are unlikely to be affected by any but extreme source bias.[6] They have the further advantage that they ordinarily can be applied on a year-by-year basis without resorting to an intermediate step of recording data on specific events and then combining them.

Our final procedures took three characteristics of strife into account: incidence, extent, and form. *Incidence* could be only roughly determined, but it is obviously important—and determinable from most sources—whether a country has several rather than several dozen riots or bombings in a year. The *extent* of strife refers to the social area affected by it. This is often not known exactly, but it was ordinarily possible to estimate whether a political strike, say, or a rebellion was confined to one small region or most of a country, to one city or several, to one group or many. Three general *forms* of strife were distinguished: turmoil, conspiracy, and internal war. Each is defined below and their principal subcategories identified. The empirical basis for the threefold distinction is provided by results of factor analyses of "conflict event" data for a large number of countries by Rummel (1963, 1965), Tanter (1965, 1966), and others. Conceptual grounds for their distinctness are argued elsewhere by the senior author (Gurr, 1970: 334-347).

Eckstein (1971: 47) proposes that the consequentiality and intensity of violence also be evaluated. Although we did not directly evaluate either one, both are partly represented by differences in strife's form and variations in its frequency. The most *consequential* kinds of strife are those with the most serious objectives—to destroy a class, an institution, or a polity. Such intentions usually are manifest in the separately categorized forms of strife we call internal wars, or major conspiracies. The *intensity* of strife events—that is the virulence of violence—varies with both frequency and form. The intensities of turmoil and of conspiracy tend to increase with their incidence—the more frequent are riots, the more violence done—and our scales assign higher scores to polities with higher incidences. Finally, turmoil and conspiracy tend to be less destructive of lives and property than are internal wars; and our summary magnitude-of-strife scores give substantially more weight to internal wars than to the other forms.

Operational Procedures

The three basic forms of strife, defined below, differ in their characteristic degree of organization, duration, intensity, and—most important—objectives and impact on the political system. The relative extent of each type of strife during a year is separately evaluated on six-point scales. The *turmoil* scale takes into account the number of events such as riots and demonstrations in proportion to population, qualified by the proportion of a country's social area affected by them. The *conspiracy* scale distinguishes between the relative severity and absolute number of events such as attempted coups and waves of terrorism. The *internal war* scale gives primary weight to the social area affected by such events as guerrilla wars and rebellions, qualified by the number of such events in progress during a year.

(1) *Extent of turmoil:* Turmoil is relatively spontaneous and unorganized strife with substantial popular participation. It involves overt confrontations between or attacks by substantial public or private groups, and typically is episodic rather than continuous. Operationally, the following kinds of events constitute turmoil: DEMONSTRATIONS: Peaceful, public gatherings (including sit-ins and marches) for the primary purpose of displaying opposition to governmental policies or authority, including student strikes but excluding political party rallies. Demonstrations organized to occur simultaneously in a number of locales are single events. Demonstrations on successive days by the same groups are counted as single events. POLITICAL STRIKES: Strikes of workers that involve more than one employer and are directed at governmental policies or authority, including governmental wage policies. RIOTS: Violent confrontations between citizens and police or troops. Riots on successive days by the same groups are counted as single events. CLASHES: Brief (less than one week), violent, and overt confrontations between members of any two communal or associational groups, e.g., political factions, economic groupings, religious or ethnic groups, student groups. Clandestine violence such as bombings and assassinations involving such groups are categorized as conspiracy (see below). PRIVATE WAR: Prolonged (more than one week), more or less continuous and overt violent conflict between members of any two of the above kinds of groups (e.g., *la Violencia* in Colombia).

These definitions are not necessarily consistent with journalistic usages, but the types are usually distinguishable in journalistic summaries. Each country is rated for each year for extent of turmoil using the following scale. Note that it is the *total relative extent of turmoil* that is rated, not separate events.

Turmoil score   *Nature of events*

5   Many demonstrations, political strikes, riots, or clashes affecting a substantial social area; *or* a private war affecting a substantial social area; *or* a private war affecting a limited social area plus some demonstrations, riots, and so on.

4   Many demonstrations, political strikes, riots, or clashes, affecting a limited social area; *or* a private war affecting a limited social area.

3   Some turmoil events, other than private war, affecting a substantial social area.

2   Some turmoil events, other than private war, affecting a limited social area.

1   A few turmoil events, other than private war.

0   No turmoil events.

Operational distinctions:

Many = at least four, or one per four million population, whichever is greater.

Some = two, or at least one per ten million population, whichever is greater.

Few = less than one per ten million population.

These distinctions are essentially arbitrary but are subject to a post hoc validity check (not attempted here) based on the smoothness of distribution of scores obtained empirically. In operational use, the distinctions ordinarily require only estimations of numbers of events, and provide a means of weighting numbers of events according to the size of the country. In France, with a population of about fifty million, at least thirteen turmoil events are needed for a coding judgment of "many." In Norway, with a population of about four million, four turmoil events are "many."

Substantial social area	The area affected by all turmoil events includes most regions; *or* more = than half the provinces; *or* a number of cities plus some rural areas; *or* most cities, or the capital city plus some other cities or regions.
Limited social area	The area affected by all turmoil events includes one or a few regions or = provinces; *or* a number of cities (less than half) but no rural areas; *or* the capital but no other locales.

(2) *Extent of conspiracy:* Conspiracy is focused and typically well-organized strife with limited participation. It ordinarily involves clandestine attacks by small private or public groups on specific targets with clearly formulated objectives. The following kinds of events constitute conspiracy; "major" and "minor" forms of conspiracy are distinguished for scoring purposes.

(a) *Minor forms:* ASSASSINATION: The (apparently) politically motivated murder or attempted murder of a major official, politician, or other public figure. Bombs sent by mail to such individuals or placed near them are assassination atttempts. Assassinations that are part of a larger campaign of clandestine attacks are "terrorism" (see below). MUTINY: Any revolt against authorities by the police or military with limited aims–i.e., aims short of replacing incumbents or overthrow of or secession from the central government. SMALL-SCALE TERRORISM: A related series of diverse attacks such as arson, sabotage, property destruction, bombings, political kidnappings, political bank robberies, beatings, executions outside the law, assassinations, sniping, or harassment. Such acts are "related" if they are perpetrated by the same group or can be inferred to be perpetrated by one or several cooperating groups on the basis of geographic and temporal association or similarity of targets. Terrorism is *small-scale* if total damage and casualties are minor or if attacks are few in number.

(b) *Major forms:* LARGE-SCALE TERRORISM: A related series of attacks as specified under small-scale terrorism. Terrorism is large-scale if total damage and casualties are substantial (multiple deaths, large or vital properties affected) *and* if attacks are numerous. COUP/PUTSCH: Any successful (coup) or unsuccessful (putsch) attempt by the military, police, or members of the ruling elite to overthrow the central government or replace its executive through the use or threat of force.

Each country is rated for each year for extent of conspiracy using the following scale. As with turmoil, it is the total relative extent of conspiracy that is rated, not separate events.

*Conspiracy
score*   *Nature of events*

5   Several major conspiracy events

4	One major conspiracy event and one or more minor conspiracy events
3	One major conspiracy event
2	Several minor conspiracy events
1	A single minor conspiracy event
0	No conspiracy events

(3) *Extent of internal war:* Internal war is well organized strife involving substantial public and private groups, accompanied by extensive violence and motivated by one faction's desire to replace or secede from a political system. The following three kinds of events constitute "internal war." GUERRILLA WAR: Hit-and-run combat between a regime and militarily organized bands of dissidents who seek to capture or destroy the regime. Guerrilla war is distinguished from revolt (below) by the circumstances of the dissidents: they are armed, organized, but usually relatively small in numbers, and operate primarily from rural base areas. So-called "urban guerrillas" are coded under terrorism, above. REVOLT/REVOLUTION: Large-scale combat between a regime and private groups who seek to capture or destroy the regime; or between two competing regimes each seeking to destroy the other. Large, nonmilitary groups play a major role on one or both sides; organized military forces and nominal members of the political elite are usually but not always found on both sides. Such revolts may be centered on national, regional, or even local governments. Examples of nationwide revolt are the Spanish "Civil War" of 1936-1939, the Hungarian "uprising" of 1956, and the Santo Domingo "revolution" of 1965. CIVIL WAR: Any armed successful or unsuccessful attempt by a substantial, regional group to secede from a government in order to form an independent or autonomous regime. The secessionist objective distinguishes civil war from guerrilla war and revolt/revolution.

Each country is rated for each year for extent of internal war, using the following scale. Internal wars often last more than a year, and are coded for each year they are in progress. The social area they affect may expand or contract from year to year, however, so that scores are not necessarily the same in successive years.

Internal War score	*Nature of events*
5	One or more internal wars, together affecting a substantial social area.
4	Two or more internal wars, together affecting a limited social area.
3	One internal war, affecting a limited social area.
2	Two or more internal wars, together affecting a very limited social area.
1	One internal war, affecting a very limited social area.
0	No internal war.

Operational distinctions

Substantial social area	=	As defined under "turmoil," above.

Limited social area	=	The area affected by all internal wars comprises several major provinces or regions; *or* several cities; *or* the capital city but no other cities or regions.

Very limited social area	=	The affected area comprises one or several rural areas; *or* one small province or region; *or* one city other than the capital; *or* several towns.

Summary scoring procedures: For each year, a total strife score is calculated by the following formula, which uses weights to estimate the relative magnitudes of the three types of strife.

$$\text{Total strife} = 1 \left(\begin{array}{c} \text{conspiracy} \\ \text{score} \end{array} \right) + 2 \left(\begin{array}{c} \text{turmoil} \\ \text{score} \end{array} \right) + 4 \left(\begin{array}{c} \text{internal war} \\ \text{score} \end{array} \right)$$

The weights are suggested by the senior author's 114-nation study of civil strife in 1961-1965. Working with relatively detailed data, "magnitude" scores were calculated for each of the three types of strife by taking the eighth root of the product of three characteristics of all occurrences of the type in the country—pervasiveness, intensity, and duration. Average scores for each type of strife are shown below, with the ratios of the turmoil and internal war scores to conspiracy (Gurr, 1968: 1107-1109).

	Score	Ratio to Conspiracy
Average magnitude of conspiracy (92 countries)	3.7	1.0
Average magnitude of turmoil (95 countries)	6.3	1.7
Average magnitude of internal war (25 countries)	15.0	4.1

The comparison suggests that the magnitudes of strife as measured above have approximately a 1 : 2 : 4 ratio to one another.

Sources: The coding procedures described above can be applied to any sources that provide reasonably comprehensive information of a journalistic or "current history" variety. Information for the quantitative coding that is summarized and discussed below was obtained largely from the *New York Times Index* listings for the twelve countries included. In many instances, this information was supplemented by reference to the *Times* itself, to summary sources such as the *New International Yearbook* especially necessary to obtain an overview of complex events like internal wars and to detailed histories. The supplementary sources also were drawn upon in preparing narrative summaries, samples of which follow for Sweden, 1927-1936, and Colombia, 1958-1967.

Strife in Sweden, 1927-1936

Compared with most other countries in Europe during this period, Sweden experienced relatively little civil disorder. But as with her European neighbors, strife events recorded for Sweden reflected the increasing polarization of politics, right and left, and labor unrest caused by the depression. Strikes were severe enough in the early thirties to have serious repercussions on the functioning and ultimate stability of the government.

A series of strikes and demonstrations in sympathy with Sacco and Vanzetti took place in Stockholm in August 1927, as they did in most European capitals. In 1928, demonstrators protested a labor bill which proposed a compulsory arbitration court for labor disputes. A large number of turmoil events occurred in 1931 as outgrowths of the economic crisis. In May of that year, strikers battled strikebreakers, and troops fired upon workers. General strikes were called in protest, and ensuing riots, which were thought to be Communist-led, resulted in many casualties. At Aadelen, where the most serious of these outbreaks occurred, and at other locales as well, troops and warships were sent in to restore order and regain control of local governments which had been taken over by Communists. (These local revolts we coded as small-scale internal wars.) The Conservative government could not effectively deal with the crisis and resigned, ushering in the long tenure of the Social Democrats in Sweden. In 1933, a large demonstration, the participants in which numbered over 50,000, was held to protest Socialist and Communist infractions of law and order, and to criticize the government for its laxity in dealing with leftist excesses (see Andren, 1961, and Elder, 1970).

Colombia, 1958-1967

The extremely high turmoil score for Colombia for these years is attributable partly to *"la Violencia."* Until the late 1950s, la Violencia had the character of a private war between supporters of the Liberal and Conservative parties. It was gradually suppressed, however, and its partisan remnants either drifted into pure banditry or provided nuclei for radical leftist guerrilla movements and "independent republics." The latter were semi-autonomous areas under guerrilla control, not often the foci of significant violence, and numbered about eleven in 1958. The "bandits," as the press referred to them, broke with the usual pattern of rural violence on occasion—for example, in September 1963—when the Army for National Liberation exploded 41 bombs in five cities in a single night. Some bands were known to be fanatically anticlerical (e.g., the Tirofijo band). According to the *Bogota Tiempo,* 727 persons were killed as a result of la Violencia in 1964 alone, but this represented a substantial decline from preceding years: between 1957 and 1964 inclusive, over 23,264 lives were lost. The staging area for much of the violence was Tolima Province, although several other departments including Valle, Huila, and Caldas apparently were involved.

Beginning in 1958, a National Front of Liberals and Conservatives governed the country, providing occasion for considerable protest and

TABLE 3
MAGNITUDES OF CIVIL STRIFE, CA. 1927-1936

Country	Magnitudes of Forms of Strife[a]			Total Magnitude of Strife[b]
	Turmoil	Conspiracy	Internal War	
Tunisia[d]	4	0	0	4
Italy	4	15	0	19
Canada	26	2	0	28
Sweden	24	0	8	32
Netherlands	32	2	0	34
Yugoslavia, 1921 1928[c]	60	10	5	75
Colombia	68	2	16	86
Germany, 1923-1932	88	11	4	103
Philippines[d]	52	2	52	106
France	86	14	20	120
Mexico	96	22	156	274
Spain, 1932-1936[c]	100	46	160	306
Means	51	10	30	91

a. Categories are defined in the text. Countries are listed in order of increasing magnitudes of strife.

b. Calculated by the formula 2(turmoil) + 1(conspiracy) + 4(internal war).

c. Scores weighted to maintain comparability with decennial scores for other country eras.

d. Not used in final quantitative analyses because of colonial status.

TABLE 4
MAGNITUDES OF CIVIL STRIFE CA. 1957-1966

Country	Magnitudes of Forms of Strife[a]			Total Magnitude of Strife[b]
	Turmoil	Conspiracy	Internal War	
Sweden	2	0	0	2
Tunisia	2	0	0	2
Yugoslavia	6	0	0	6
Netherlands	10	0	0	10
Germany	6	10	0	16
Canada	18	6	0	24
Spain	26	10	0	36
Mexico	38	3	8	49
Italy	40	14	0	54
Philippines	22	6	36	64
France, 1959-1968	56	22	20	98
Colombia, 1958-1967	78	12	32	122
Means	25	7	8	40

a. Categories are defined in the text. Countries are listed in order of increasing magnitudes of strife.

b. Calculated by the formula 2(turmoil) + 1(conspiracy) + 4(internal war).

disorder. Supporters of the dictator ousted in 1957, General Rojas Pinilla, were repeatedly involved, along with other extreme Conservatives who did not support the Front. Pro-Castroites were active on the left. Pro- and anti-Rojas groups demonstrated and rioted when Rojas was brought to trial in October 1958. Several attempted coups were rumored in 1958, one of which came to light in May, when four members of the interim junta were kidnapped. In October 1961, the civilian government of the Liberal president, Lleras Camargo, quashed a putsch by right-wing army troops, alleged supporters of Rojas Pinilla, and declared a state of siege that lasted nearly twelve weeks. In 1963, despite the fact that a Conservative president was in office, Rojas supporters several times demonstrated on behalf of their leader and in November attempted to storm the government palace.

During the middle 1960s, the surviving "republics" and guerrilla bands were reduced in number but were increasingly and genuinely revolutionary. Actions involving these groups are coded internal war. Communist guerrillas based near the Venezuelan border operated during the middle 1960s. In 1964 and 1965, terroristic activity by these and similar groups began to increase in and near the cities, particularly in the form of bombings and kidnappings. In 1966 and 1967, there were a few small-scale guerrilla attacks on police posts and patrols, attributed by the government to Communist bands.

Turmoil continued in the middle 1960s. Widespread and serious student demonstrations occurred in 1964 against the latest candidate of the National Front, the Liberal Lleras Restrepo, and continued in 1965. The demonstrations, in conjunction with growing terrorism, prompted the declaration of a state of siege in mid-1965. In May 1966, during the heat of the election campaign, students again demonstrated, urging a boycott of the May elections. They also marked the one-year anniversary of the siege by burning United States flags and raising guerrilla standards. In October, they stoned the motorcade which carried newly elected President Lleras and his guest, John D. Rockefeller. No turmoil was reported in 1967, however (see Dix, 1967: ch. 13).

Comparisons

Summary measures of magnitudes of strife, by polity by decade, are shown in Tables 3 and 4. Two kinds of internal comparisons of these data can be made: by country across time, and among types of strife for all polities combined. We also have data with which to estimate reliability and validity.

Cross-time comparisons: None of the countries was completely free of strife in either era, but strife declined substantially between the earlier and later periods, by more than half the mean "total magnitude" scores. The decline characterizes all forms of strife, internal war most of all. The question as to whether strife declined systematically for all countries is answered by the correlation coefficients in Table 5, which show only weak relations between levels of strife in the two eras. Levels of turmoil 1927-1936, for example, correlate .35 with turmoil in 1957-1966, a relationship far below the .05 level of significance. In other words, though average levels of strife declined markedly, the decline was considerably greater in some countries than in others. In two countries, Italy and Colombia, strife increased.

All-polity comparisons: Table 6 shows that magnitudes of the different forms of strife are moderately to strongly associated with one another, in comparisons spanning all polities.[7] Magnitudes of conspiracy and internal war are more closely interconnected than turmoil is with either of them. All three component measures are strongly correlated with total magnitude of strife. Total strife and all its component measures except turmoil have strongly skewed distribution, each with a few very high values.

Reliability and validity: Data are available to evaluate both the reliability and validity of the strife scores. We assessed the reliability of the coding procedures used by comparing the results of two independent codings of

TABLE 5
CROSS-TIME COMPARISONS OF MAGNITUDES OF
STRIFE, n=12[a]

1927-1936	1957-1966			
	Turmoil	Conspiracy	Internal War	All Strife
Turmoil	**35**	36	27	37
Conspiracy	17	**33**	-21	09
Internal war	19	03	**08**	15
All strife	27	19	12	**24**

a. Product moment correlation coefficients x 100. None of the r's are significant at the .05 level for n=12.

TABLE 6
COMPARISONS OF FORMS OF STRIFE FOR
ALL POLITIES, n=21[a]

	Turmoil	Conspiracy	Internal War	All Strife
Turmoil	100	63[b]	65[c]	86[c]
Conspiracy		100	77[c]	83[c]
Internal war			100	95[c]

a. Product-moment correlation coefficients x 100. Also see note 6.

b. Significant at the .05 level using a one-tailed test.

c. Significant at the .01 level using a one-tailed test.

eight polities. The r's, shown in the first column of Table

high, ranging from .79 for internal war to .90 for total

ices are somewhat greater for the specific forms of strife

because of slight modifications made in some category

levelopment of supplementary distinctions, and the use of

add... es for the second, final coding.

Several other measures of strife are available for evaluating the validity of our results. Two such comparisons are shown in Table 7. In the first, our data (totals for 1961-1965 only) are shown to correlate quite highly with the senior author's "magnitude of strife" measures for the same period (Gurr, 1969). The latter rely on much different and more precise measures obtained from more detailed sources. The second comparison is with Nesvold's scaled scores for specifically political violence for the 1948-1965 period (Feierabend et al., 1969). The correlations here are lower but still significant in three of four instances; the differences are probably due partly to scaling procedures, partly to the fact that Nesvold's data cover a longer time span. These comparisons suggest that the method devised and used in the present study for estimating magnitudes of strife gives results consistent with others that have recently been used. Equally important, it is considerably more efficient, at least for gross comparisons, because the requisite information is more readily collected and scaled.

LEGITIMACY

Legitimacy refers to the extent that a polity is regarded by its members as worthy of support. This is not the same as citizens' actual compliance with laws and directives, but refers to a basic attitude that disposes them to comply in most circumstances. On the conceptual and empirical importance of the distinction see Eckstein (1971: 50-52). These sentiments of worthiness, or legitimacy, are a crucial criterion of performance because they provide the psychological cement of a polity. To the extent that legitimacy is low or nonexistent, people are likely to support and obey authorities only out of fear or convenience, which means that rulers must either rely expensively on coercion or risk political collapse when crises require popular privation or mobilization.

It is necessary to distinguish among the scope and objects of legitimacy. No polity is likely to command the loyalty of all its citizens all the time; what is crucial for high performance is that no large or vital segment of the population remain alienated for any length of time. The objects of people's feelings of legitimacy—or illegitimacy—often are distinguished analytically. Almond and Verba (1963: 101) speak of citizens' feelings toward government officials ("output affect") and their feelings about participation ("input

TABLE 7
RELIABILITY AND VALIDITY OF 1957-1966
STRIFE MEASURES

	Criterion Measures		
	Recoding 1957-1966 (n=8)[a]	Gurr 1961-1965 Strife (n=12)[b]	Nesvold Political Violence 1948-1965 (n=12)[c]
Turmoil	87[e]	91[e]	61[d]
Conspiracy	85[e]	70[d]	58[d]
Internal war	79[e]	(not incl.)	25
Total strife	90[e]	93[e]	62[d]

a. Product-moment r's (x 100) between decennial strife data in Table 4 and data from an independent coding, by different coders, for eight countries.

b. Product-moment r's between country scores summed for 1961-1965 only, and magnitude-of-strife scores constructed by weighting measures of strife pervasiveness, intensity, and duration, reported in Gurr (1969: 489-91). Operational definitions of turmoil and conspiracy differ somewhat between the two studies.

c. Product-moment r's between decennial strife data, 1957-1966, and Guttman-scaled political violence scores for 1948-1965 constructed by Nesvold (Feierabend, Feierabend, and Nesvold, 1969: 513).

d. Significant at the .05 level.

e. Significant at the .01 level.

affect"). We distinguish here among four objects of legitimacy: the political community, the regime, its incumbents, and its policies (see Easton, 1963, 1965; Gamson, 1968). These attitudes are likely to have a hierarchy of salience for most citizens of most countries. Some people in every country presumably regard some governmental policies and directives as illegitimate, and in most democracies such attitudes are so commonly expressed that they seldom are thought to be serious unless and until they are manifest in attacks on the legitimacy of those who issued them—the incumbents—or in attacks on the legitimacy of the institutions and procedures by which they are made. In extremis, feelings of illegitimacy may generalize from policies to incumbents to the regime and ultimately to the political community itself, as they did for many American Southerners in the decades before 1861. This hierarchy of attitudes may be considered from the opposite perspective as well: if a segment of a country's people does not accept the validity of the political community, they are unlikely to regard as legitimate its policies, incumbents, or institutions. Though such hierarchies do not necessarily take this order, the importance of the conceptual distinctions makes it desirable to distinguish operationally among the objects of legitimacy, as is done below. We focus principally on the legitimacy of the political community and the regime, taking into account evidence about the legitimacy of incumbents only in monolithic and no-party polities; in democracies, it was not usually possible, using our sources, to distinguish sentiments about the legitimacy of incumbents from the partisan attitudes of conventional political competition.

relationships between legitimacy and the durability and civil order ⸮ns of performance can also be postulated. The legitimacy of a system ⸮ more to promote its durability than vice versa. A highly legitimate polity is much more likely than an illegitimate one to be able to muster the "inputs" needed to defend it against crises that might otherwise terminate it. Moreover, civil strife in a highly legitimate system is likely to be less intense and less consequential, insofar as it involves public groups, than in illegitimate polities. A polity's lack of legitimacy may of itself be a grievance that inspires violent attacks on the regime (see Gurr, 1970: 186-187). This is not to imply that high legitimacy precludes political violence, much less communal violence. Illegitimate policies or incumbents in otherwise highly legitimate polities are especially likely to inspire sharp protests at those policies and leaders, because they threaten people's general sense of identification with the polity. Ceterus paribus, a less legitimate polity tends to have a higher threshold of tolerance for violent opposition to specific policies and leaders, but less resistance to internal wars—which frequently are fatal to the polity. Another perhaps unnecessary qualification is that neither civil order nor durability is primarily determined by legitimacy; both are also affected by decisional efficacy as well as by conditions not formally included among the performance dimensions, notably the occurrence of severe societal strain. Moreover there also are feedback effects whereby prolonged civil order and durability enhance future legitimacy. The longer a system endures at internal peace, the more likely are the symbols and attitudes of legitimacy to be passed on unquestioningly from one generation to the next (see Merelman, 1966).

Operational Approaches

Most definitions of legitimacy and related concepts like "system affect" (Almond and Verba, 1963) and "political allegiance" (Lane, 1962) regard it as a psychological variable, as we do here. This helps account for the paucity of attempts to assess it cross-nationally: comparable data on attitudes are not easily or cheaply collected. Other approaches to the concept emphasize the aggregate consequences or causes of such attitudes; Lipset (1960: ch. 3), for example, equates legitimacy with one of its presumed consequences, political stability, and Bwy (1968), in a study of Latin America, indexes the concept with a measure of one of its presumed causes, the degree of political democracy in each society. A recent study by the senior author combines measures of presumed causes *and* consequences of feelings of legitimacy: legitimacy is assumed to vary positively both with the degree to which political institutions are of indigenous rather than foreign origin, and with their durability (Gurr, 1968).

Attributing legitimacy to the presence of institutions of a particular kind, irrespective of variations in political culture, is at best questionable and at worst an imposition of the observer's values on the societies he is studying. Indexing legitimacy by measures of the extent of civil order or durability is inappropriate for this study because we wish to determine the relationships among strife, legitimacy, and durability. Survey research techniques appear to be a relatively precise and direct way of ascertaining legitimacy, but were foreclosed to us for reasons of finance and access. A pragmatic and attractive alternative we considered was to examine evidence of *compliance* with governmental directives in the countries we studied. Compliance is not identical with legitimacy, for citizens may regard directives as proper and worthy of obedience but still not obey because of the dictates of self-interest; or they may regard them as quite illegitimate but still obey on pain of sanctions or out of habit. Still, the degree of compliance with laws governing taxation, conscription, school attendance, voting, and other such state-regulated or state-directed activities should indicate something of a government's legitimacy. But relevant and comparable evidence on compliance was not available in sources to which we had access.

The operational procedures we finally devised are based on the extent, intensity, and persistence of what we call *illegitimacy manifestations,* that is, overt and publicized kinds of phenomena that are likely to occur only if the people involved in them feel that some aspects of their political system are illegitimate. Four general categories of such phenomena are shown in Table 8, including various forms of civil strife; organized, nonviolent extremist activity; repressive action by regimes in response to actual or suspected oppositional activity; and various kinds of verbal and other symbolic attacks on regimes and, in monolithic systems, their incumbents. Some other kinds of events and conditions might also be regarded as evidence of illegitimacy sentiments; the list in Table 8 guided the collection of the data reported below.

Three objects of illegitimacy sentiments were operationally distinguished:

(a) *The political community:* the existence and boundaries of the state itself.
(b) *The regime:* the organization of the state, including its fundamental institutions and processes of elite recruitment, decision-making, administration, and adjudication.
(c) *Incumbents:* the individuals occupying the higher superordinate positions, including the chief executive, ministers or cabinet officers, national representatives, heads of the judiciary, and, in one-party states, the party leadership.

The basic assumption underlying the scales and scoring procedures outlined below is that the fewer the illegitimacy manifestations in the era studied, the higher is legitimacy. Conversely, the greater their number, intensity, persistence, and scope, the lower is legitimacy. The serious conceptual shortcoming of the approach is that the legitimacy dimension is bipolar, varying from a negative pole through a zero point to a positive pole, of which only the zero-to-negative segment is fully represented by "illegitimacy manifestations." For a general discussion of this problem, and some approaches to its resolution, see Eckstein (1971: 54-64).

An operational rather than conceptual problem is posed by authoritarian polities. In most of them, the expression of illegitimacy sentiments is more sharply inhibited than in pluralistic polities, usually by coercive means. We have taken three steps to correct for this. One is to weigh heavily any repressive regime policies toward actual and potential opposition groups; this is done for all polities, authoritarian and otherwise, but such policies are more often used by authoritarian regimes. A second is to evaluate the intensity of illegitimacy by reference to the most intense act of opposition in a period; in a hypothetical comparison, a decade of demonstrations by left-wing opposition in the Netherlands would register a lower intensity than a single wave of bombings by Spanish Communists. Our third adjustment is to register attacks on incumbents as manifestations of illegitimacy only in authoritarian polities. Such attacks, physical and symbolic, are more likely indicators of deeply felt rejection of the polity in authoritarian than in democratic states.

A second operational problem is the sparseness of news and historical sources for some countries and eras. We may, for example, overestimate the legitimacy of the Colombian polity during 1927-1936 by comparison with the thoroughly reported French Third Republic. We think that our reliance on the more intense manifestations helps corrects for this; disruptive attacks are more likely to be reported than are mild ones. But for this reason, and those cited in the two preceding paragraphs, we think that legitimacy is less adequately operationalized than the other performance dimensions.

Operational Procedures

The initial step in gathering information on illegitimacy was to identify the major categories or groups in a country engaged in intense opposition: separatist regions, political parties both legal and illegal, economic organizations, the military, and the like. This was done using a variety of historical studies. Then the historical studies as well as news sources and chronicles were searched for information on the objectives of each group and a chronology made of its oppositional activities. This information was used to determine the principal object(s) of illegitimacy sentiments, and to evaluate their *intensity, persistence,* and *scope.* Two measures of *intensity* of illegitimacy are described below: one takes into account the type of sentiment or objective expressed, the other the form in which it is expressed. Feelings of legitimacy vary across time, sentiments toward the political community probably being least susceptible to change and sentiments toward incumbents most variable. *Persistence* is indexed by the number of years in which manifestations directed against a particular object occur in the period being studied. The *scope* of a manifestation is the proportion of a population

TABLE 8
LIST OF ILLEGITIMACY MANIFESTATIONS

Type of Illegitimacy Manifestations	Typical Object(s)
(1) Overt Strife:	
Secessionist civil wars	Political community
Anti-government riots	
Anti-government demonstrations	
General (political) strikes	
—if directed against the regime	Regime
—if directed against specific political leaders	Incumbents
Guerrilla wars	Regime
Coups d'etat, whether or not successful:	
—if actors demand or attempt institutional renovation	Regime
—if actors demand or attempt replacement of elite only	Incumbents
Anti-government terrorism	Regime or incumbents
Political assassinations	Regime or incumbents
(2) Organized Extremist Oppositional Activity (nonviolent)	
Plots:	
—if reportedly aimed at dissolving the state (rare)	Political community
—if reportedly aimed at changing the regime (common)	Regime
—if reportedly aimed at assassinating or otherwise replacing elite members	Incumbents
—if no object specified	Regime (by inference)
Separatist organizations active, legally or illegally	Political community
Extremist political parties or organizations active, legally or illegally	Regime and incumbents
(3) Governmental Repressive Measures	
Purges (arrests of large numbers of political figures)	Regime (by inference)
Mass arrests (of rank-and-file political opponents or suspected opponents)	Regime (by inference)
States of emergency, martial law, suspension of constitutional guarantees, at the national, or regional, or local level	Regime (by inference)
Governmental action against political challengers, e.g. physical attacks on political opponents or their property, cancellation or manipulation of elections	Incumbents (by inference)
(4) Symbolic Oppositional Activity	
Widespread attacks by news media and/or public figures:	
–demands for dissolution of the state (rare)	Political community
–demands for constitutional change, institutional change, change in power distribution among social and political units, etc.	Regime
–attacks on incumbent political leaders	Incumbents
Unusually high nonparticipation in elections	Regime or incumbents
(5) Miscellaneous	
Large-scale flows of political refugees	Political community or regime
Negative votes to constitutional referenda	Regime
Formation of private paramilitary organizations for group defense or assault	Regime or incumbents
Widespread sabotage of implementation of governmental policies	Regime or incumbents

inferred to share the feelings of illegitimacy manifest in it. Scope is a crucial qualification to intensity and persistence, since most political systems can function quite well when only a few of their members are intensely disaffected, but work poorly or collapse under the attacks of many.

Intensity of illegitimacy: Each group is coded for each period by object and according to the illegitimacy sentiments of greatest intensity, as defined in the two sets of scales below. Conditions reflecting less intense opposition are not coded because of the Guttman-type scaling relationship assumed—i.e., illegitimacy sentiments of a given level of intensity are assumed to imply the presence of sentiments of lesser intensity.

(1) *The nature of illegitimacy sentiment*
    (a) *Political community as object*

Score	Nature of sentiment or objective
10	Dissolution of the country into multiple, autonomous components.
6	Separation of one component of the country from the remainder so that it can function autonomously, or be associated with another state.
3	Grant a substantially greater measure of autonomy, but not complete separation, to one or several components of the country.

    (b) *Regime as object of illegitimacy sentiment*

Score	Nature of sentiment or objective
10	Basic transformation of both institutions and processes.
8	Basic transformation of either institutions or processes.
6	Major revision of both institutions and processes.
4	Major revision of either institutions or processes.
2	Diffuse or general dissatisfaction with regime, specific object not clear.

    (c) *Incumbents as object of illegitimacy sentiment* (applied to authoritarian polities only)

Score	Nature of sentiment or objective
10	Attacks on the appropriateness of most or all top decision makers.
8	Attacks on the appropriateness of the chief executive and some other decision makers.
6	Attacks on the appropriateness of most or all of a class of decision makers; e.g., most representatives, most ministers, *or* diffuse or general dissatisfaction with incumbents at several levels.
4	Attacks on the appropriateness of the chief executive.
2	Attacks on the appropriateness of one or two specific decision makers other than the chief executive.

Note: Attacks are actions or statements that directly and clearly challenge the legitimacy of the decision maker(s). Criticisms in the course of normal political debate ordinarily are not attacks in this sense.

(2) *The form of illegitimacy sentiment*
    (a) *Political community as object*

Score	Type of event or condition
10	Overt, organized, violent activity by groups attempting to secede from or dissolve the country—e.g., secessionist civil wars like the American Civil War and separatist movements like that of the Karins and Kachins of Burma.

8   Unorganized, violent activity (riots) by groups demanding the dissolution of the country.

6   Evidence of clandestine activity directed at dissolution of the country including separatist terrorism or plots, and repressive prophylaxis by the regime in the form of purges and mass arrests.

4   Emigration motivated by hostility toward the country per se, especially among minority group members—e.g., Turks leaving the Balkans after the dissolution of the Ottoman Empire.

2   Direct, symbolic attacks on the propriety of the existence of the country—e.g., demands for Scottish independence on grounds that Scotland is not properly part of Britain.

(b) *Regime as object*

Score   *Type of event or condition*

10   Overt, organized, violent activity, other than by members of the elite, designed to transform the regime—e.g., the Hitler putsch of 1923, the Hungarian Revolution of 1957, the Cuban Revolution of 1956-1958, and so on.

8   Evidence of clandestine activity directed at transforming the regime or some part of it, including plots and repressive prophylaxis by the regime—e.g., South African policies toward opponents of apartheid in the mid-1960s, the Communist-supported plot to overthrow the Iranian monarchy in 1950, and so on.

7   Rioting by those demanding institutional change—e.g., riotous strikes by French Communists in the 1930s, some U.S., French, and German student riots of the 1960s, and so on.

6   Active but nonviolent presence of legal or quasi-legal organizations advocating regime transformation—e.g., the Communist Party in France and Italy, and the Muslim Brotherhood in the UAR during the 1950s; *and* demonstrations and peaceful general strikes by advocates of regime transformation.

5   Peaceful removal or deposition of a regime widely regarded as illegitimate—e.g., the popularly supported military coup that ended the Rojas dictatorship in Colombia in 1957.

4   Direct, symbolic attacks on the propriety of the regime—e.g., demands in the French Fifth Republic that the balance of executive and assembly power be changed, attacks on political recruitment processes that exclude minority group members, and so on; *and* violent clashes between political groups advocating different institutional patterns.

2   General, diffuse rejection of the institutions or basic procedures of government expressed, for example, in voting support for parties advocating transformation, opinion surveys, widespread editorial or scholarly opinion, and so on.

(c) *Incumbents as objects* (applied to authoritarian polities only)

Score   *Type of event or condition*

10   Overt, large-scale, violent activity directed against specific incumbents—e.g., violent demonstrations against U.S. cabinet officials or the president, riots against the military junta in the Sudan in 1964, and so on.

8   Clandestine violence against incumbents—e.g., successful and attempted assassinations and bombings directed against specific decision makers, and repressive prophylaxis by the regime against groups said to be plotting against incumbents.

6   Nonviolent, demonstrative strife against specific incumbents—e.g., street demonstrations against President de Gaulle's visit to Le Havre in 1965, and so on.

4   Direct, symbolic attacks on the appropriateness or legitimacy of specific decision makers, including resort to prescribed but infrequently used sanctions—e.g., impeachment proceedings against elected officials in the United States, German attacks on Chancellor Erhard in 1965-1966 because of his asserted weakness in response to internal and external policy crises, and so on.

2   General, diffuse rejection of incumbents expressed in massive and vocal opposition to a specific incumbent or incumbents, widespread editorial or scholarly opinion that an incumbent is not suited for office, and so on.

Scope of illegitimacy sentiments: Illegitimacy sentiments are inferred to exist among the group or groups that are directly involved in the events specified above, and among those who support the acts or who are said to be represented by those who carry out the acts. Often no more than an educated guess is possible. The following examples, not from the data collected, illustrate some guidelines:

(a) In the American Civil War, the proportion of population in which illegitimacy sentiments are inferred is the population of the Confederate States as a percentage of total population. Similarly, the Kurdish rebellion in Iraq can be said to reflect illegitimacy sentiments on the part of all Kurds.

(b) A series of anti-regime plots and several attempted rebellions occurred in Bolivia in the 1950s, supported by members of the upper and middle classes who were opposed to the revolution of 1952. One can infer, on the basis of country knowledge, that perhaps half the upper and middle classes were alienated by the revolution and were sympathetic to the plots—i.e., substantially less than ten percent of the population.

(c) The Indian Communist Party, which advocates substantial changes in the Indian political system, obtains (hypothetically) fifteen percent of the vote in national elections; its voting support can be used as a measure of the scope of illegitimacy sentiments represented by the party's activity.

A variety of evidence of this and other kinds is recorded, relative voting support being the most useful datum for most Western democracies. The relative size of the group is coded on a 10-point scale, a score of 1 being assigned if the proportion was 10% or less of the total population, 2 if the proportion was between 11 and 20%, etc. Scoring is based on the largest group in which a particular type of sentiment was manifest, which was often considerably larger than the group represented in the most intense illegitimacy event or condition. For example, relatively few sympathizers and members of the Nazi Party took part in antiregime rioting and assassinations of officials in the late 1920's and early 1930's, but the "scope" score assigned to Nazi activities is based on the maximum relative voting strength of the party before Hitler assumed the Chancellorship.

Persistence of illegitimacy manifestations: The persistence score is the number of years during each ten-year coding period in which an event or condition occurred. Events like antigovernment demonstrations and intense hostility toward a particular incumbent are typically episodic. The activities of separatists and of extremist parties are more often persisting ones, with manifestations occurring every year in a decade. The scoring convention employed for organizations of the latter sort is to score 1 for each year in which the sources used made specific reference to their oppositional activity. For example, autonomist sentiment may have been present among the people of Brittany throughout the 1957-1966 decade, but our sources referred to overt autonomist activity in only one year, hence the persistence score assigned is 1. In Italy during the same decade, by contrast, separatism in the Alto Adige was manifest in reports of demonstrations, terrorism, or police prophylaxis for every year of the decade; persistence = 10.

Summary Scoring Procedures

These are complex. After initial coding, our data for each country were lists of groups manifesting illegitimacy sentiments, each group with diverse objects and separate Intensity (I), Persistence (P), and Scope (S) scores. We "summed" these scores both horizontally and vertically. Horizontally, we determined for each group "magnitude of illegitimacy" scores; then, combining groups, we horizontally summed again to get separate "magnitude of illegitimacy" scores *by object*—i.e., political community, regime, and incumbents. (Information on the illegitimacy of incumbents in nonauthoritarian polities was not used in the final scoring, for reasons noted above.) Vertically, we added down weighted sums of I, P, and S characteristics of illegitimacy, irrespective of their group or object. Finally, from the summary I, P, and S scores so obtained we summed horizontally again to get a *total magnitude of illegitimacy* score. Three of these sets of scores are listed in Tables 9 and 10: illegitimacy by object (cols. 1–3); illegitimacy by characteristic I, P, and S (cols. 4-6); and total magnitude of illegitimacy (col. 7). Detailed scores by group are available on request (see note 1).

The arithmetical procedures used in combining scores are described below.

Magnitude of illegitimacy scores by group: The *group illegitimacy score* is the sum of the "intensity : object," "intensity : form," and "persistence" scores multiplied by the "scope" score. The first three scores all represent aspects of the intensity of feelings directed at a particular object; the "scope" score is used to weight the intensity score according to the approximate proportion of the population sharing such feelings.

Magnitude of illegitimacy scores by object: For actions directed at each specific object, the *intensity* of illegitimacy scores is weighted by their relative scopes:

TABLE 9
MAGNITUDE OF ILLEGITIMACY CA. 1927-1936

Country	Magnitude of Illegitimacy by Object						Total Magnitude of Illegitimacy[b]
	Political Community	Regime	Incumbents[a]	Intensity	Persistence	Scope	
Netherlands	0.0	2.3	(1.7)	7.3	8	.1	1.5
Sweden	0.0	3.6	(5.2)	5.5	7	.2	2.5
Colombia	0.0	3.8	(5.6)	5.0	9	.2	2.8
Canada	0.0	5.1	(2.4)	5.0	7	.3	3.6
Mexico	0.0	9.7	(10.6)	7.1	10	.4	6.8
Italy	2.1	4.7	5.3	21.5	10	.3	9.5
Yugoslavia, 1921-1928[c]	10.2	12.2	(12.1)	15.6	10	.6	15.4
France	1.8	16.7	(18.6)	12.6	10	.7	15.8
Germany, 1923-1932	4.6	21.4	(19.0)	14.1	10	.8	19.3
Spain, 1932-1936	5.2	23.2	(25.6)	17.5	10	.8	22.0
Means	2.39	10.27	10.61	11.12	9.1	.4	9.92

a. Not included in "intensity," "persistence," "scope," or "total magnitude" scores except for Italy.

b. Countries are listed in order of decreasing apparent legitimacy.

c. Scores are weighted to maintain comparability with decennial scores for other country eras.

TABLE 10
MAGNITUDE OF ILLEGITIMACY CA. 1957-1966

Country	Magnitude of Illegitimacy by Object						Total Magnitude of Illegitimacy[b]
	Political Community	Regime	Incumbents[a]	Intensity	Persistence	Scope	
Netherlands	0.0	1.3	(1.4)	4.3	4	.1	0.8
Mexico	0.0	2.0	(7.1)	5.7	9	.1	1.5
Philippines	0.0	2.1	(8.8)	6.5	8	.1	1.5
Sweden	0.0	2.2	(0.0)	3.5	4	.2	1.5
West Germany	0.0	2.4	(6.7)	7.0	10	.1	1.7
Tunisia	0.0	3.0	1.1	13.5	4	.2	3.5
Yugoslavia	1.6	1.6	1.1	12.0	10	.2	4.4
Canada	1.8	6.4	(2.2)	9.0	10	.4	7.6
Colombia 1958-1967	0.0	10.7	(4.8)	5.7	10	.5	7.9
France 1959-1968	1.0	9.3	(13.7)	11.1	10	.4	8.4
Spain	2.1	5.8	3.6	14.7	10	.4	9.9
Italy	2.4	10.9	(12.4)	11.6	10	.6	13.0
Means	0.74	4.81	5.24	8.72	8.3	0.28	5.14

a. Not included in "intensity," "persistence," "scope," or "total magnitude" scores except for Yugoslavia and Spain.

b. Countries are listed in order of decreasing apparent legitimacy.

$$OI = \frac{\Sigma \left(\frac{IO + IF}{2} \cdot S \right)}{\Sigma S}$$

where IO = intensity:object score of each group, IF = intensity:form score of each group, and S = scope score of each group.

The persistence of illegitimacy of each object, P, is the number of years in a decade in which any illegitimacy events occurred directed against a specific object. For example, if military plots against a regime were reported in four of ten years and opposition politicians vehemently denounced the legitimacy of cabinet procedures during two of the same years and three others, the persistence score for attacks on the regime is seven.

The *scope* of actions directed at each object is the deflated sum of group scope scores, OS—i.e., a sum that eliminates any double-counting of population segments counted in two separate groups, and the cumulative effect of inflated scope estimates of tiny oppositional groups. For example, workers who are counted in two groups of scope scores—as members of an extremist political party and also as residents of an autonomous region—are counted only once in the "object" scope score. Similarly, two autonomous movements supported respectively by two or three percent of a population would each have group scope scores of .1 but in a deflated total are given a combined score of .1 rather than .2.

The object illegitimacy score, OM, is calculated similarly to the group summary score:

$$OM = OS(2 \times OI + P).$$

For example, if the regime total intensity score is 7.0, persistence is 5, and the deflated scope is 0.3, object illegitimacy = 0.3(14 + 5) = 5.7.

The object intensity scores are double-weighted in the formulae vis-à-vis persistence because the intensity with which illegitimacy sentiments are expressed is conceptually more important than the frequency of their expression. The latter varies situationally according to such extrinsic factors as the nature of the regime and opportunities for collective action. Operationally, intensity is also more precisely measured.

Total magnitude of illegitimacy, all objects: The *total intensity* of illegitimacy, ΣI, is the sum of the object intensity scores, OI. The *total persistence,* ΣP, of illegitimacy is the number of years in the decade in which any illegitimacy events against any objects occurred. The *total scope* of action, ΣS, is the deflated sum (discussed above) of the object scope scores, OS. The *total magnitude of illegitimacy,* ΣMIL, is calculated by the following formula:

$$\Sigma S(\Sigma I + \Sigma P)$$

It will be noted that the total magnitude of illegitimacy is always equal to or less than the sum of the magnitude scores by object, and in some instances is less than the highest object illegitimacy score.

In addition to summary scores, narrative interpretations of legitimacy were prepared for each country era. Sample narratives are given below for Spain, 1931-1936 (1931 was not included in our scoring because it was a year of transition), and Canada, 1957-1966.

Spain, 1931-1936

This was one of the most turbulent eras of Spanish political history, a period in which none of a succession of leaders and governments was able to establish or maintain substantial popular acceptance. The monarchy under Alfonso XIII, and the military directorate through which it ruled, collapsed in 1930-1931 in the face of growing challenges to its legitimacy. The republic established in its place could not secure the enduring support of any major political group except by resorting to policies that incurred the intense hostility of other groups. The center political groups on which the republic attempted to base its legitimacy largely vanished between 1931 and 1936 under an assortment of cross-pressures that splintered them into fragments in dispute over a variety of issues. A substantial minority of the population was polarized into groups on the left and right, neither of them loyal to the institutions of the republic except insofar as they could transform them to their own purposes, both of them hostile to its incumbents, who did not represent their own faction. The ultimate result of these divisive and complex pressures was the civil war, which began in 1936, when the forces of the right attacked the occupants of the institutional shell of the republic.

The groups on Spain's political left included anarchists, syndicalists, communists, and radical socialists, groups which jointly had the support of perhaps a tenth of the Spanish population during the later years of the monarchy, but which by 1936 were mainstays--with many liberals and socialists--of the republic's Popular Front government that won 49% of the vote in national elections. (In 1933 the left alone won 20% of the vote.) All had demonstrated their rejection of the monarchy and dictatorship in repeated and repeatedly suppressed antigovernment general strikes, riots, and occasional terrorism through 1931. The anarchists and syndicalists continued equally violent opposition to the leaders and institutions of the republic, culminating in a widespread but unsuccessful revolutionary (and separatist) uprising in October 1934. Only in 1935 and 1936 did the extreme left parties accept the parliamentary rules of the game, in what seemed a pragmatic rather than an ideological decision that led to the creation of the Popular Front and nominal leftist acceptance of the legitimacy of republican institutions, though not its remaining center-right incumbents.

The political right during the republic included groups ranging from proto-fascists, like Primo de Rivera's Spanish Falange, and monarchists to agrarians to Gil Robles' Catholic Party (Accion Popular), almost all of which joined the Rightist Union in 1936 in electoral opposition to the Popular Front, getting 44% of the vote. During most of the period, extreme rightist as well as left-wing groups engaged in sporadic anti-regime violence. The Catholic Party vehemently challenged the legitimacy of anticlerical legislation and of incumbents who supported it but supported and participated in republican institutions until the Popular Front victory in 1936. Subsequently, extremist groups on the right became involved in escalating violence with the left that coalesced with the July revolt of the army.

At the core of the political center were the left and radical (right) republicans and the moderate socialists, who formed the first republican governments. Center parties did not represent significant illegitimacy sentiments during the republic, except occasionally against some incumbents over policy issues, but declined in electoral support from 50% in the 1931 municipal elections to 36% in 1933 and less than 10% in 1936.

One of the most fundamental challenges to the legitimacy of the Spanish political system was posed by the separatists and ultra-federalists, who in extremis attacked not merely the regime and its incumbents but the existence of the political community itself. Autonomy movements were strongest among the Basques and Catalans, jointly about 15% of the population; weaker movements in Galicia, Valencia, Alicante, and Andalusia were largely controlled by the republic. The tactics used included conventional political participation after 1931; agitation and violent turmoil throughout the period; and attempted secession of the Basques and Catalans during the 1934 insurrection, which was suppressed only after severe fighting, especially in Barcelona.

The military was an independent source of challenges to governmental legitimacy throughout the period. Intense resistance to the republican regime and its incumbents was reflected in a number of garrison revolts in 1931-1932 by rightist opponents of the new republic. But far the most consequential was the generals' revolt in July 1936 that began the civil war and ultimately destroyed the republic.

In summary, political groups representing most Spaniards at one time or another between 1931 and 1936 opposed both incumbents and regimes with the most violent of means and desires for the most fundamental kinds of political changes, motivated by a host of conflicts over land, religion, class, and politics. A substantial minority of Spain's inhabitants, some 15%, did not regard themselves primarily as Spaniards and sought autonomy, some of them by violent means. Manifestations of regime and incumbent illegitimacy occurred in every year of the period, as they did of political community illegitimacy (separatism). By the scores which quantify these generalizations, the Spanish republic had less legitimacy than any other polity examined in this study.

Canada 1957-1966

The most serious challenge to the Canadian political system came from elements of the French-Canadian population in Quebec Province. Their demands ranged from greater provincial control to total separation of the province from Canada and the creation of a new nation. Quebec separatist sentiment at the beginning of the decade was muted; it intensified sharply so that by 1966 provincial leaders were vigorously demanding funds and jurisdictional autonomy for major changes in educational, economic, cultural, and social policies. The most extreme manifestations of nationalism were demands for separatism expressed in terrorist activity and violent demonstrations, which occurred in six of the ten years. A survey conducted in 1963 showed that 13% of French Canadians sought autonomy; 43% wanted to stay united to the dominion; 23% were undecided and 21% were uninformed of proposals to separate. In all, we judged that a tenth or less of the total Canadian population rejected outright the legitimacy of the political community.

Also reflected in the scoring was a muted but long-standing regional resentment with the federal government, based partly on the belief, widespread in the prairie and western provinces, that some federal economic policies were discriminatory. Under more stressful conditions in the 1930s, this dissatisfaction stimulated serious challenges to the legitimacy of the federal regime. The lack of equally overt challenges in the 1950s and 1960s does not necessarily signify that the federal regime was strongly legitimate. During this period, provincial governments sought in a variety of ways to reverse the trend to centralization, their efforts reaching a peak in 1964. One of the effects was a substantial weakening of the effective authority of the federal government. Generally, it seems most appropriate to regard the federal government of Canada as weakly or partially legitimated in the prairie and western regions, as well as in Quebec. This is reflected in our scoring judgment that the regime was the subject of widespread illegitimacy sentiment of a low intensity level.

General dissatisfaction with incumbents also characterized much of the decade. Both Conservative Prime Minister Diefenbaker and his successor, Liberal Prime Minister Pearson, were widely regarded as ineffectual, not only by the respective political oppositions but by some of their own supporters. A series of scandals involving public officials, and unusually vehement attacks on persons and policies in parliament, also occurred. The legitimacy of incumbents suffered; so, as a consequence, did the legitimacy of parliament itself. This is not reflected in the coding because of our decision to exclude incumbent illegitimacy from summary scores in democratic polities.

Comparisons by Country

The summary measures by country in Tables 9 and 10 show a substantial overall decline in illegitimacy, hence an inferred average increase in legitimacy, between 1927-1936 and 1957-1966. The summary score averages decline by nearly half, comparable to the decline in magnitudes of strife over the same period remarked in the second major section. Changes in the rank order of countries were also large, except at the extremes of the scale. The Netherlands and Sweden were both highly legitimate in both eras, while France and Spain were near or at the opposite pole in both; the rankings of the polities of most other countries shifted markedly. Rank-orderings are somewhat misleading at the "illegitimate" end of the continuum, as France illustrates: the Third Republic was the third most illegitimate polity of the first era, as was the Fifth Republic in the second era, but the magnitude of illegitimacy of the Fifth Republic was about half that of the Third Republic. The greatest absolute declines in legitimacy between the two eras occurred in Colombia and Canada; the greatest absolute increases occurred in Spain and Yugoslavia.

Quantitative evidence that the change in legitimacy between the 1930s and the 1960s was not consistent in its effects appears in Table 11. The top half of the table shows almost no association between magnitudes of illegitimacy, by object or total, between the two decades. The only, partial exception is an expected one: the illegitimacy of the political community, based on autonomist and separatist activities, correlates .42 with itself over time. Separatism is a more persisting source of overt hostility than grievances about particular regimes or their incumbents.

The cross-time comparisons between the pairs of measures of Intensity and Persistence in the lower half of Table 11 are significant, the Scope correlation is not. The Persistence comparison is uninteresting: it reflects the high proportion of "10" scores in both decades. The Intensity comparison is decidedly interesting, however: it suggests that there is some continuity within political cultures in the relative intensity with which incumbents and regimes are challenged—considerably more continuity than there is in the proportion of population mobilized by such challenges. The observation is all the more striking because seven of the ten nations in the statistical comparison underwent polity transformations between the two decades.

Comparisons by Polity

Statistical comparisons of the various measures of illegitimacy for all polities combined are summarized in Table 12. Comparison of illegitimacy by

TABLE 11
CROSS-TIME COMPARISONS OF MAGNITUDES OF
ILLEGITIMACY, BY OBJECT AND CHARACTERISTIC, n=10[a]

1927-1936	Object of Illegitimacy, 1957-1966			
	Political Community	Regime	Incumbents	Total
Political community	42	-24	-11	09
Regime	20	-09	26	10
Incumbents	20	-01	29	16
Total	40	00	33	26
1927-1936	Characteristics of Illegitimacy, 1957-1966			
	Intensity	Persistence	Scope	Total
Intensity	77[c]	46	32	54
Persistence	56[b]	63[b]	09	29
Scope	43	58[b]	-18	-01
Total	74[c]	57[b]	02	26

a. Product-moment correlation coefficients x 100. Tunisia and the Philippines are excluded because of their colonial status in the first era.

b. Significant at the .05 level for n=10.

c. Significant at the .01 level for n=10.

object shows that regime illegitimacy is the dominant component of the summary score, whereas challenges to the legitimacy of the political community tend to vary independently of the legitimacy of either the regime or its incumbents. An interpretation was suggested above. The high correlation of incumbent illegitimacy with the "regime" and "total" measures suggests that it too is a good indicator of overall illegitimacy, though we did not use it as such except in authoritarian polities. The correlation also suggests that it can be excluded without loss of the summary scale's discriminant capacity.

The relative contributions of the separate Intensity, Pervasiveness, and Scope indicators to total magnitude of illegitimacy are determinable from the correlations in the lower half of Table 12. The correlations are not sufficiently strong to warrant discarding one or more of the indicators. The total magnitude of illegitimacy, though, is considerably more a function of Scope than of the other two characteristics, because of the multiplicative relationship built into the scoring.[8] This suggests that the Scope indicator could be used as a sole index of legitimacy. However, the Scope scores are the least reliable of the three, depending on often arbitrary judgments about the size of groups hostile to a regime or incumbents. The preferable alternative is to relate the Scope indicator additively to the Intensity and Persistence indicators in future analyses, or perhaps to rely only on the latter two.

Comparison of strife and illegitimacy: One requirement of measures of conceptually independent variables is that they be operationally distinct from

TABLE 12
COMPARISON OF ASPECTS OF ILLEGITIMACY FOR
ALL POLITIES, n=21[a]

By Object	Political Community	Regime	Incumbents	Total Magnitude
Political community	100	61[b]	53[b]	76[b]
Regime		100	89[b]	94[b]
Incumbents			100	83[b]

By Characteristic	Intensity	Persistence	Scope	Total Magnitude
Intensity	100	61[b]	52[b]	76[b]
Persistence		100	51[b]	56[b]
Scope			100	85[b]

a. See note 7.
b. Significant at the .01 level.

one another. The above measures of illegitimacy may seem to violate this requirement by relying in part on characteristics of strife, which we have treated separately in the preceding major section. There are two answers to this possible objection. Analytically, the variables *are* distinct, but causally they are closely linked: both are aspects of the performance of political systems and expected to vary rather closely. Operationally, the summary measures of strife and of illegitimacy take into account different aspects of strife; in indexing strife we were concerned with its form and with the extent of its overt manifestation, whereas in indexing illegitimacy we used the form of strife to help score one component of one indicator of the intensity of hostility, taking into account its objectives rather than its extent. Empirically, the two sets of measures have moderate to strong correlations, as Table 13 shows. The relations between turmoil and conspiracy, on one hand, and incumbent and regime illegitimacy on the other, are strongest. The magnitude of illegitimacy of the political community is only weakly related to the strife measures. Overall, the summary strife and illegitimacy measures correlate only .57. The overall pattern of the correlation matrix tends to justify treating the variables, as indexed in this study, as causally connected, rather than operationally contaminated.

DECISIONAL EFFICACY: INDICES AND COMPARISONS

Decisional efficacy is the extent to which polities make and carry out prompt and relevant decisions in response to political challenges. The centrality of decisional efficacy to performance seems self-evident (see Eckstein, 1971: 65-78). A polity which is unable to make prompt and relevant decisions is unlikely to be able to accomplish any task, even to

TABLE 13
COMPARISONS OF MAGNITUDES OF STRIFE AND
ILLEGITIMACY, 21 POLITIES

Magnitudes of Illegitimacy	Magnitudes of Strife			
	Turmoil	Conspiracy	Internal War	Total
Incumbents	77[b]	79[b]	55[b]	73[b]
Regime	82[b]	75[b]	49[a]	71[b]
Community	34	39[a]	10	25
Total	66[b]	72[b]	36	57[b]

a. Significant at the .05 level.
b. Significant at the .01 level.

preserve its own existence. The disruption of civil order, for example, is a common consequence of delayed or irrelevant decisional responses to challenges. The outcome of civil strife similarly depends in part on governmental decisions or nondecisions. Legitimacy can be created and enhanced or destroyed according to the kinds and promptness of decisions made. Ultimately, the durability of a polity depends substantially upon the capacity of incumbents to make a continuous flow of appropriate decisions about a multiplicity of issues, large and small, in response to demands of citizens, external challenges, and their own perceptions of the requirements of survival for society and polity. The most obdurate difficulties posed by decisional efficacy are not conceptual but operational.

Operational Approaches

Our initial approach to operational measurement was to identify decisional challenges in each country, defining them as "intense demands on behalf of large or strategic groups that the government take action to protect or enhance their own or other members' value positions," and then to evaluate how promptly and with how much or little conflict relevant decisions were made to deal with the challenges. Extensive pretesting showed that challenges could be identified and their magnitude assessed, albeit with some difficulty, but reliable standards for evaluating decisional responses to them could not be devised. Part of the difficulty was insufficient information, but more critical was the variability of the "promptness" and "appropriateness" of responses according to both the nature of the specific challenge and the traditions of each country. We also suspected that such countries as Sweden and the Netherlands were largely free of major challenges because of the efficacy and foresightedness of more-routine and less-visible decisions. Finally, we abandoned the attempt to devise impartial and universally applicable criteria for comparing challenge responses, though still recognizing the feasibility and desirability of making case, and ultimately, comparative studies of such decisions.

In the face of these difficulties, we decided to concentrate on the efficacy of decisions about two issues that arise recurrently for every polity: budget-making and the internal allocation of authority. All national governments must decide periodically—usually annually—how to allocate their resources among various claimants, and all have at least nominal procedures by which incumbents attain, maintain, and transfer their authority. These are functional requisites of system survival: the body politic that does not satisfy them does not last long. Moreover we can ask with considerable comparability how long such decisions are in the making and how much elite conflict and procedural instability they occasion. They provide a litmus-like test from which we can tell a great deal about any divisiveness and inefficiency among the elite and also forecast its capacity to deal with episodic crises. Information was separately collected and scaled for the efficacy of budget-making and the maintenance of authority by the procedures described in the immediately following two sections. The results are discussed and compared in the final section.

Operational Procedures: The Efficacy of Budgetary Decisions

Every polity in our study had formally prescribed procedures for formulating and passing budgets, including the formulation by various agencies of budget estimates or requests; the coordination of such claims by the executive; and the ratification of the final budget by the legislature, with or without debate and modification. We asked three kinds of questions about the efficiency of actual budgetary practices, as described in various news and country sources:

(1) Is the budget "on time?" Formulation of a budget after the fiscal year to which it is applicable begins is ordinarily a symptom of conflict or at least inefficiency. The later its passage, and the more extreme the strategems resorted to in securing its passage, the lower is budgetary efficacy, as scored on the following scale. The general rationale for the scoring procedure is discussed below.

Scale for evaluating promptness of budgetary decision:

Score	Timing of Budgetary Decision
+2	Budget passed or decreed before the fiscal year begins without unusual delay, subsequent major revision, or resort to special procedures.
+1	Budget passed or decreed before the fiscal year begins, but is subject to substantial revision during the course of the fiscal year.
+1	Budget *not* passed or decreed before the fiscal year begins, but is routinely late, the previous year's budget being customarily extended to cover the intervening period.

0	Budget is passed before the fiscal year begins only by resort to an emergency or special session of the legislature.
0	Budget is passed within two days after the fiscal year begins.
-1	Budget is passed between two and thirty days after the fiscal year begins.
-1	Budget is passed before the fiscal year begins but only by resort to unusual strategems—e.g., changing the fiscal year, executive resort to sanctions (threatened vote of confidence, use of decree power), and so on.
-2	Budget is passed more than one month after the fiscal year begins.
00	No basis for judging (coded only if information is so scant that nothing can be inferred about when the budget was passed).

Note on coding: Each country is scored for each year for the lowest appropriate score. If budgets are determined biannually, the score for a nonbudget year is the same as for the preceding budget year.

(2) Are budgetary procedures stable? A recurrent response to paralyzing debate over budgetary issues is tinkering with budgetary procedures, in some cases a complete overhaul of the procedures and even of the entire regime in which they are embodied. The following scale for this variable treats any reported change in budgetary procedures from one year to the next as prima facie evidence of inefficiency, but qualifies the judgment according to the degree of elite opposition to the changes.

Scale for evaluating stability of budgetary procedures:

Score	Type and Extent of Change	Status of Change
+2	No change from previous year's procedures.	No opposition to procedures from decisional elite reported—i.e., from legislators, cabinet officers, or equivalent officials.
+1	No change from previous year's procedures.	Procedures reportedly challenged as inappropriate or unconstitutional by segments of the decisional elite.
+2	Minor procedural changes—e.g., change in fiscal year, form of budget, priority of consideration of items, and so on.	No reported elite opposition.
+1	Minor procedural changes.	Elite opposition to changes reported.
0	Major procedural changes—e.g., imposition of limit on debate followed by executive decision if legislative approval not granted; or requirement of presidential approval before budget is submitted for legislative discussion.	No elite opposition reported.
-1	Major procedural changes.	Elite opposition to changes reported.
0	Resort to emergency procedures—e.g., budget issued by executive decree after inability of legislature to pass it.	Constitutional sanctions exist for emergency procedures, and elites either sanction resort to them or apparently acquiesce.
-2	Resort to emergency procedures.	No constitutional sanction for procedures, or elite opposition reported, or both.

0	Major, permanent, or semipermanent change in budgetary decision-making authority—e.g., transfer from legislature to executive as part of new constitution or as condition of rule by leaders of a coup.	Approved by legislature or by referendum, without reported elite opposition.
-1	Major, permanent or semipermanent change in budgetary decision-making authority.	Not formally approved by legislature or referendum, but no reported elite opposition.
-2	Major, permanent or semipermanent change in budgetary decision-making authority.	Elite opposition to change reported.
00	No basis for judging (code only if information is so scant that it cannot be inferred even that routine procedures were followed).	

Notes on coding: Each country is scored for each year for the lowest appropriate score—e.g., if a major procedural change is made without opposition (= 0) and subsequently a major transfer of authority is made without opposition (= −1), the annual score is −1. If budgets are determined biannually, as in Spain, the score for a nonbudget year is the same as for the preceding budget year. The scale does not include all conceivable types of changes in budgetary procedures and forms of opposition to change. Scores for other situations should be assigned judgmentally.

(3) Is there sharp elite dissension over budgetary issues? Debate over budgetary and related fiscal issues often reaches disruptive intensity—for example, when ministers resign or governments fall over economic issues. The greater the intensity of dissension, as indexed on the following scale, the lower is budgetary efficacy. It will be noted that the kinds of dissension incorporated in the scale can occur without necessarily affecting budgetary timing or procedural stability, which justifies this assessment of dissension separately from the other budgetary variables.

Scale for evaluating budgetary dissension

Score	Nature of Dissension
+2	The budget is known or inferred to have been deliberated in the executive or legislature, but no sharp debates concerning it are reported.
+1	Sharp, intense conflict reported within the executive, the legislature, or between them, over budgetary issues, but no elite breaks occur. Conflict is "sharp" if it involves, for example, unusually vehement attacks by the opposition; threat of sanctions (to withdraw from a coalition, to use decree powers); delaying or sabotaging parliamentary tactics; civil service strikes to oppose fiscal policies; and so on. Dissension may focus on specific budgetary items, on general policy orientations as reflected in the budget, or on procedures of budgetary preparation.
0	No budgetary deliberation in either the executive or legislature, a condition most likely to be inferred in situations in which temporary decree power for the budget is assumed by the executive.
-1	Elite breaks occur over budgetary and related economic issues—e.g., resignation of a finance minister in opposition to fiscal policy, resignation of a party from a coalition to oppose budget policies (if the resignation does not bring down the government), demotion or purging of a major official over economic issues, and so on.

-2   Elite collapse occurs over budgetary and related economic issues, for example, a fall of government or a coup d'état inspired partly by an economic crisis, such as inability to decide on a budget, to resolve budgetary deficits, or to solve a fiscal crisis, and so on.

00   No basis for judging (coded only if there is no information on the nature or existence of the deliberation process).

Note on coding: Each country is scored for each year for the lowest appropriate score. If several elite breaks or elite collapses occur in a year over budgetary issues, only one such event is scored.

A fourth characteristic of budget-making, the extent to which budgets are deliberated, was originally included. It was deleted during reanalyses, on conceptual grounds that extent of open deliberation is a function of political style rather than performance, and on empirical grounds that the measure did not correlate well with the other measures.

Scaling and scoring procedures for budgetary efficiency: The three basic questions posed above were asked in the abstract and information relevant to each question then collected for eleven countries from a variety of sources, principally the *New York Times.* The kinds of events recorded under each rubric were then cataloged and judgmentally ordered, combined, and assigned scale values according to the apparent degree of "inefficacy" they represented. Scores were then given to each polity on each variable for each year for which information was available.

Symbolic and scoring considerations both suggested the consistent use of 5-point scales ranging from +2 to −2 for each variable. The +1 categories all represent relatively minor deviations from "pure" efficacy, insufficient by themselves to warrant a judgment that a polity's performance was seriously impaired. The negatively scored categories, however, all represent major if not fatal failings. (Subsequent "consensual validation" discussions suggest that some of the −1 and −2 conditions for budget and authority efficacy should have more substantially negative scores.) *Annual scores* for each country were determined by averaging all 0, +1, and +2 scores (excluding 00 scores, which represent "no information") and subtracting from them the sum of negative scores. *Decennial scores by variable* were calculated for "timing," "procedural stability," and "elite dissension" by averaging the annual scores for each variable. These scores are listed in Tables 14 and 15, as are *summary decennial scores,* constructed by averaging the summary annual scores. The effect of the annual-score procedure is to give relatively high summary scores for countries, and country-years, in which budgetary efficacy is at or above the mid-point of the scales, but to penalize them heavily for the most serious kinds of conflict and decisional failure. One consequence is that the variable scores alone, since they are not so weighted, exhibit somewhat less variability than the summary scores.

TABLE 14
EFFICACY OF BUDGET FORMATION CA. 1927-1936[a]

Country	Timing	Procedural Stability	Elite Dissension	Summary Score[b]
Sweden	2.00	2.00	1.90	1.97
Italy	2.00	1.40	1.60	1.60
Canada	0.30	2.00	1.90	1.17
Mexico	1.12	1.43	1.12	1.15
Netherlands	1.00	1.90	1.00	1.12
Colombia	0.57	0.80	1.56	0.90
Spain, 1932-1936	1.40	1.20	1.20	0.87
Yugoslavia, 1921-1929[c]	0.80	1.00	0.00	0.30
Germany, 1923-1933	-0.30	0.60	-0.40	-0.82
France	-0.80	1.20	-0.70	-1.05
Means	0.81	1.35	0.92	0.72

a. Variables are defined in the text. Countries are listed in order of decreasing budgetary decisional efficacy.

b. The average of annual scores, not directly derivable from the summary scores by variables.

c. Data are missing for 16 of 29 variable/year scores for Yugoslavia.

Operational Procedures: Maintenance of Authority

Every polity has means for perpetuating its authority, and most have some means by which the wielders of authority periodically are confirmed or replaced in office. The processes by which the top decision makers, the decisional elite, are chosen and maintain themselves afford many opportunities for conflict among actual and aspiring decision makers. These processes of the maintenance of authority afford one test of the efficacy of a political system: we assume that efficacy is high to the extent that the formation, maintenance, and replacement of governments is accomplished without disruptive conflict. Some conflict characterizes most elite interactions; it is disruptive to the extent that it causes the paralysis or breakdown of the system.

The operational problem posed by this argument was to assess comparatively the efficacy with which political systems maintain authority. This required three inputs: a generalized conceptual map of the processes of authority maintenance; a body of empirical information on the nature and frailties of these processes in particular systems; and a set of indices for rating the extent to which each process was efficient or disrupted by conflict. That is the reconstructed logic of the procedure. As with evaluation of budgetary efficacy, the empirical information was collected first, following a general set of categories. Systematic examination of this information suggested the general conceptual map, scalable variables, and operational definitions of categories arrayed along each variable. The problem throughout was to devise

TABLE 15
EFFICACY OF BUDGET FORMATION CA. 1957-1966[a]

Country	Timing	Procedural Stability	Elite Dissension	Summary Score[b]
Mexico	1.67	2.00	2.00	1.89
Spain	2.00	2.00	1.50	1.83
Sweden	1.60	2.00	1.70	1.68
Colombia, 1958-1967	1.67	1.72	1.11	1.50
Italy	0.90	2.00	1.30	1.40
Yugoslavia	2.00	2.00	1.30	1.37
France, 1959-1968	1.67	1.60	0.30	1.23
Philippines[c]	1.00	n.d.	1.20	1.22
Netherlands	1.00	2.00	0.80	1.02
Canada	0.20	2.00	0.70	0.72
West Germany	-0.50	2.00	1.30	0.58
Means	1.29	1.93	1.21	1.33

a. See note a, Table 14. Tunisia is not included for lack of adequate information.
b. See note b, Table 14.
c. Data are missing for 21 of 30 variable/year scores for the Philippines.

concepts and measures appropriate to assessing authority maintenance in diverse systems, including no-party, one-party, and multiparty presidential and cabinet systems.

The general conceptual map of the processes of authority maintenance is shown in Figure 1. The boxes signify events or conditions; the arrows represent processes. Only some of the conditions and sets of processes ordinarily characterize a particular polity; over a long period, all of them may occur in one system.

Events and conditions of authority maintenance: ELECTION: national, direct, or indirect election of all or all of one set of national legislators or the chief executive, or both, including uncontested elections and legislative election of a chief of state or chief executive; and including candidate selection, election preparations, and the campaign (if any). GOVERN-MENTAL FORMATION: the assemblage of a working group of top executive decision makers, typically a cabinet, sometimes a council, special committee, or junta, or the establishment of a working relationship between an extant group and a new chief executive. INCUMBENCY: the life span of the government, until validated or terminated. A government's incumbency may last through various conflicts, considerable turnover in members, and limited structural or functional reformations until it ends in an *election* (above), *governmental fall* (below), or *polity termination* (below). GOVERNMENTAL FALL: the resignation or removal from office of the government as a body or, in an autocratic system, the death, resignation, or removal of the autocrat. POLITY TRANSFORMATION: a major structural or functional transformation of the polity—e.g., the replacement of a presidential with a dictatorial system or a multiparty with a one-party system. For a comprehensive operational list, see p. 35. These transformations may be accomplished by incumbents as in Germany, 1933-1935 and Cuba, 1959-1962; by dissident members of the elite as in Colombia in 1957 or by revolutionaries.

The Processes of Authority Maintenance

The numbered definitions below refer to the numbers shown on Figure 1.

(1) The *periodic election cycle,* in which incumbents are subject to periodic elections either at fixed intervals or at a time of their own choosing, which lead to either (1a) continuation of the government in office (in a presidential system it may so continue even if the opposition scores a legislative victory), or (1b) replacement of the government by victorious opponents or a new coalition. (A third outcome not separately shown in Figure 1, because of its rarity, is regime termination as a direct result of elections—e.g., the 1962 military coup in Peru because election results were politically unacceptable.)

(2) The *decision crisis cycle,* in which a government or chief executive resigns or is dismissed under pressure, typically because of inability to deal with a legislative issue, leading to either (2a) new elections and the formation of a new government (including instances in which an interim government is formed until elections can be held), or (2b) formation of a new government without resort to elections.

(3) *Polity termination,* which may occur as a result of (3a) the fall of a government—e.g., when such a fall precipitates a coup; or (3b) the formation of a government—e.g., when a chief of state assumes personal rule and dissolves a legislature because of its inability to form a government; or (3c) most commonly, by direct intervention in or self-transformation of an incumbent government (see the definition of polity transformation above).

(4) *Polity establishment,* the formation of a new polity with substantially reformed characteristics. Such a polity may be created directly, or in a process that may

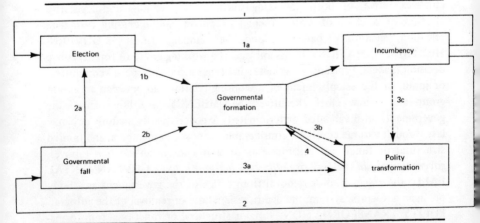

Figure 2: PROCESS OF AUTHORITY MAINTENANCE

include formation of an interim regime, constitutional revision, the holding of elections, and then the formation of a new government, according to the terms prescribed for the new polity.

Variables of authority maintenance: Seven variables of authority maintenance were identified, scaled, and scored from the information gathered on processes and conditions. The processes themselves were scored according to the degree of inefficacy they appeared to represent. Three of the processes were then evaluated in more detail for evidence of inefficacy. For elections, when held, the stability of procedures and degree of elite dissension were scaled. For government formation, whether or not following elections, procedures and dissension were similarly scaled. Finally, scales were constructed to summarize the extent of procedural and personnel changes in governments during their incumbency. The scales and scores for each category on them are summarized below.

Processes: The first, descriptive step in analysis of the data for each country was to indicate which processes shown in Figure 1 occurred during the year, in sequence, using the alphanumeric descriptors shown in the figure. If a government remained in office without election, fall, or termination, the descriptive code is 0. If an election led to the resignation of a government even though it did not lose its legislative majority, it is coded 1b, "election followed by government formation," rather than 2b, "governmental fall."

This is a complex, hypothetical example: a cabinet falls on a vote of confidence; a new one is directly formed but falls shortly thereafter; legislative elections are held, and yet a third government is formed, but is unacceptable to the chief of state, who assumes sole power with military backing and rules by decree through the end of the year, pending constitutional revision and new elections. The year would be descriptively coded 2b, 2a, 3b, and our coding for the polity would end with its termination. If we were to begin coding with the new polity formed after elections, the initial code would be 4 (but not 1a or 1b, since the transformation process 4 comprises all steps including elections in forming a new polity).

The following scale is used for scoring the degree of continuity or disruption represented by the various processes; the score for each year is the sum of scores for all recorded events.

Code	Score
1a, 1b	+2
2a, 2b if not more than a total of two occurrences in the 10-year period*	+1
0	00
4	0
2a, 2b if a total of three or four occurrences in the 10-year period*	0

2a, 2b if a total of five or more occurrences in the 10-year period.* -1

3 -2

*If more than one governmental fall occurs in a year (2a and/or 2b), the score is −1 for each occurrence, however many occur in the decade.

Elections: For each year in which there were national elections for any set of offices, their procedural stability and any consequent dissension among the elite is scored using the following scales. If no elections were scheduled or held, each scale is scored 00. Some relevant events, like party splits, may occur in the year before a national election; all changes and dissension associated with an election are coded for the election year. If events in more than one category on a scale occurred, or if more than one national election were held in a year, only the lowest appropriate score on the scale is assigned.

Stability of Electoral Procedures

Score	Conditions or Events
+2	No changes in election procedures, no new restrictions on opposition, elections held on time.
+1	Minor revisions in electoral procedures–e.g., constitutional amendment of election rules; brief delay of elections to establish election machinery; elections set ahead of conventional time; minor new restrictions on partisan activity, and so on.
0	Institution of elections for an office or body for the first time.
00	No elections scheduled or held.
−1	Substantial revisions in electoral procedures–e.g., change from a unicameral to bicameral legislature before elections; constitutional revision to permit chief executive to run again; substantial new restrictions on partisan activity; banning of significant opposition party; and so on.
−2	Basic change in electoral procedures–e.g., scheduled elections not held; all opposition parties banned; incumbents attempt to or do sabotage electoral results; and so on.

Elite Dissension over Elections

Score	Conditions or Events
+2	No significant new alignments among political forces or divisiveness within the ruling party or coalition, or among the opposition, prior to the election.
+1	Prospects of election lead to *elite realignments*–e.g., the formation of new parties, or coalitions; individual defections from one party to another, and so on.
00	No elections scheduled or held.
−1	Prospects of election lead to moderate elite fragmentation or substantial increase in intensity of opposition–e.g., divisive disagreements or temporary splits in the ruling group or party; desertion of a coalition party into hostile opposition; breakup of a coalition; splits in opposition parties; threatened or actual boycott of an election by a party or faction, and so on.
−1	Illegitimate sanctions or force are used in the election campaign–e.g., opposition candidates are jailed or terrorized by the regime; competing factions make sporadic use of violence, either in clashes, terrorism, or assassination; considerable corruption occurs at the polls; and so on.
−2	Both of above occur–i.e., moderate elite fragmentation/substantial intensification of opposition, *and* illegitimate sanctions or force used.

−2   Election prospects or results lead to *intense and persistent elite fragmentation*—e.g., enduring splits in a ruling party; revolt or civil war by disaffected candidates, and so on (note that a breakup in a coalition before elections, even if permanent, is coded −1).

Formation of governments: For each year in which a government was formed, scores are assigned for the procedural stability of the process and the degree of elite delay and dissension in forming the government. If the formation of a government overlapped two calendar years, it is scored for the year in which the government was finally formed. If several governments were formed in a year, the total number of days in their formation is summed and used as the basis for the "elite delay and dissension" scale, in conjunction with the *most serious* level of dissension reported during any of the formations.

A number of conditions other than elections can require the formation of governments or the functional equivalent, for example the decision of a majority party to reform the government; falls of cabinets; resignations or death of a chief executive, chief executive-elect, or head of state; basic changes in the structures or processes of the regime, whether by external or internal means; transfer of power from a colonial to an indigenous government; and so on. All such events are included in the scoring, but note that the last two by definition can occur only at the birth of a new polity.

Procedures of Government Formation

Score	Condition
+2	No change from conventional or constitutionally prescribed procedures, no immediately consequent crisis.
00	No government formation necessary or attempted during year.
−1	Head of state or interim government resort to exceptional procedures of government formation—e.g., use of "crisis cabinets," resort to decree power because of undue delay in government formation, and so on.
−2	The process or immediate outcome of government formation leads to a major crisis in the procedures or structure of government—i.e., the threat or actuality of polity termination.

Elite Delay and Dissension in Governmental Formation

Score	Condition
+2	*Governmental formation is prompt and no elite dissension is reported.* Formation is "prompt" if governmental operations are not delayed for more than four days; in a presidential system there usually are no delays since new governments are typically formed during the time between elections and inauguration; in a cabinet system delays are considerably more varied. Functional equivalents of "prompt" governmental formation are a lack of delay in selecting a new head of state or chief executive after a death or resignation; "smooth" transfer of power from a colonial to indigenous authority or from a dictator or junta to a new democratic system; the prompt resumption of power by an autocrat after the death of his successor; and so on.

	Duration of Delay	Elite Dissension
+1	Four days or less.	Moderate dissension (defined below).

+1	Five to twenty days.	No dissension reported.
0	Four days or less.	Intense dissension (defined below).
0	Five to twenty days.	Moderate dissension.
−1	Five to twenty days.	Intense dissension.
−1	More than twenty days.	Moderate dissension.
−2	More than twenty days.	Intense dissension.
00	No governmental formation, *or* no information on duration of delay.	

MODERATE ELITE DISSENSION is signified by such conditions as reports of intraparty conflict over cabinet formation; a minority party's temporary refusal to join in order to secure greater concessions; conflictive negotiations among former or prospective coalition partners; conflict between a newly chosen chief executive and head of state; refusal of selected cabinet officer to serve; and so on. INTENSE ELITE DISSENSION is signified by such conditions and events as attempts by a coalition partner to sabotage governmental formation; a serious and persisting split in a party attempting to form a government; refusal of a major opposition party to accept or cooperate with a proposed government–e.g., by boycott of or prolonged disruptive tactics in the legislature; violent conflict between candidates for chief executive or head of state; jailing, exile, or execution of rival candidates for executive authority; and so on.

Governmental incumbency: Whether or not elections, falls, formation of governments, or polity terminations occur during a year, various kinds of changes in the personnel and procedures of the decisional elite can occur, with or without serious conflict. Two kinds of such conditions are coded: the extent of structural and procedural changes in the government *other than* those associated with elections and governmental formation (such changes are relatively uncommon); and the extent of elite pressure on and consequent change in the personnel of the government, changes ranging from cabinet reorganizations and resignations to governmental collapse. Both of these variables are coded for each year, the lowest score prevailing for years in which several categories of events occur.

Structural and Procedural Changes in Governmental Incumbency

Score	Change
+2	No changes reported.
+1	Minor structural or procedural changes–e.g., new extra-cabinet executive position created to deal with a problem area; new consultative committee established at the top executive level; procedures for considering bills changed moderately to minimize conflict; and so on.
00	No information on governmental incumbency, no basis for assuming it was stable.
−1	Substantial changes–e.g., unusual pact between a government and an opposition party to keep the government in power; emergency powers given to coalition government, chief executive, or head of state by the legislature or cabinet; the balance of political representation is substantially changed when autocrat reforms cabinet; and so on.
−2	Basic changes–e.g., the major parties form a long-term coalition to avoid crisis; regime transformation, including such steps as replacement of opposing incumbents, suspension of constitutional rights, thorough constitutional revision and so on; the inception of a civil or revolutionary war that ultimately results in polity termination (coded for each year in which the war is in progress), and so on.

Note that polity termination is coded here only when it occurs during a period of incumbency rather than in response to the fall or formation of governments.

Personnel Changes and Elite Conflict in Government Incumbency

Score	Personnel Changes	Elite Conflict
+2	None; or individual resignations of chief executive or minister(s) for personal reasons; routine shuffles in cabinet personnel; and so on.	No evidence of unusual pressure for changes from opposition or conflict within government.
+1	No resignations or personnel changes.	Unusual pressure from the opposition (e.g. criticism or investigation of a minister; no-confidence motions; impeachment proceedings; widespread demands for resignation, and so on.
+1	No resignations or personnel changes.	Government or chief executive assumed to be under unusual new pressure from opposition because of warnings or sanctions against opposition groups (characteristic of autocratic regimes).
0	No resignations or personnel changes.	Government or chief executive under unusual pressure from some members of the government, its own party, or a coalition member—e.g., coalition partner attacks or withdraws; member of government publicly attacks other members; rival in party pressures chief executive to resign, and so on.
0	One or two members of the government (other than the chief executive) resign or are dismissed.	Under opposition pressure.
0	Government resigns—e.g., to give executive a "free hand" in military or economic crises, to form a stronger coalition, and so on.	No evidence of unusual opposition pressure or internal conflict.
−1	One or two members of the government (other than the chief executive) resign or are dismissed.	Under internal pressure.
−1	Resignation of chief executive or a number of members of the government; or major governmental reshuffling.	Under opposition pressure.
−2	Resignation of chief executive or a number of members of the government; or major governmental reshuffling.	Under internal pressure.
−2	Government falls (coded only once even if several falls occur during the year).	Under opposition or internal pressure.
00	No information on governmental incumbency, no basis for assuming a lack of change or conflict.	

TABLE 16
DECISIONAL EFFICACY: MAINTENANCE OF AUTHORITY CA. 1927-1936[a]

Country	Elections			Govt. Formation		Govt. Continuation		Summary Score[b]
	Processes	Procedures	Dissension	Procedures	Dissension	Procedures	Changes	
Canada	2.00	2.00	2.00	2.00	1.00	1.90	1.60	1.73
Netherlands	1.33	2.00	2.00	2.00	1.50	2.00	1.30	1.68
Sweden	1.00	2.00	1.33	2.00	1.50	2.00	0.60	1.50
Italy	2.00	1.50	2.00	2.00	2.00	2.00	0.60	1.28
Mexico	2.00	1.33	1.33	1.40	1.00	1.30	-0.10	1.10
Colombia	2.00	2.00	1.25	0.50	-0.50	0.50	-0.37	0.81
Germany, 1923-1933	-1.55	1.33	-0.17	1.00	-1.00	0.55	-1.64	-0.73
France	-2.11	1.60	1.80	1.33	-0.11	1.10	-1.70	-0.76
Yugoslavia, 1921-1929	-1.67	1.67	0.67	0.88	-1.11	0.57	-1.89	-1.09
Spain, 1932-1936	-4.00	2.00	1.00	0.50	-0.50	0.40	-1.20	-1.83
Means	0.10	1.74	1.32	1.36	0.38	1.23	-0.28	0.40

a. Variables are defined in the text. Countries are listed in order of decreasing efficacy in the maintenance of authority.

b. The average of annual scores, not directly derivable from the summary scores by variable.

Almost all the events and conditions used as examples in the foregoing scales are taken from the evidence collected on the countries in our sample. The cutting points at which quantitative variables such as duration of delay in governmental formation and the number of cabinet resignations are divided into more general categories are similarly suggested by the distribution of a large number of instances identified in these countries.

Scoring Procedures for Authority Maintenance

The information for establishing and scoring the scales was obtained from the same sources used for budgetary efficacy. The *New York Times* again provided the richest and most detailed information, when interpreted in the frameworks provided by political histories and analyses of the countries studied. *Annual summary scores* for each country were calculated by averaging the "processes" score with the average of the other six variables. *Decennial variable scores* are averages of the annual scores for each and are shown in Tables 16 and 17, along with *summary decennial scores,* which are the average of the annual summary scores. It may be noted that a special weighting of negative scores was not used for authority maintenance as it was for budgetary efficacy; the heavy weighting of the "processes" score, with its negative component extending beyond -2 for chronically unstable governments, is functionally equivalent. The use of the -2 to $+2$ scale also facilitates comparison with the budgetary efficacy scores.

Narrative accounts of budgetary decision-making and the maintenance of authority were prepared for polities in our sample. Three examples appear below.

The Philippines, 1957-1966: allocation of authority: Presidential elections took place every four years—1957, 1961, 1965—though transitions from one administration to another were accompanied by a good deal of conflict. The two traditional parties, Nationalist and Liberal, are "cadre" parties, their leaders largely dependent upon personal followings. Defections from one party to the other are regular features of Philippine politics. For example, a third force in Philippine politics was briefly established with the landslide election of Magsaysay to the presidency in 1953. This force mostly dissolved with his death in 1957, but dissident elements survived. Some of these former Magsaysay followers (MPM) and rebels from the Nationalist and Liberal Parties formed the Grand Alliance in 1959. In 1960, this group united with the Liberal Party in a successful challenge to the reelection of Nationalist President Garcia.

The turnover of personnel in incumbent administrations is also high. Many cabinet and subcabinet appointments are made to pay off political debts, and substantial rotation is practiced to maximize the number of beneficiaries. In

TABLE 17
DECISIONAL EFFICACY: MAINTENANCE OF AUTHORITY CA. 1957-1966[a]

Country	Elections			Govt. Formation		Govt. Continuation		Summary Score[b]
	Processes	Procedures	Dissension	Procedures	Dissension	Procedures	Changes	
Mexico	2.00	2.00	0.00	2.00	2.00	1.90	2.00	1.94
Spain	2.00	2.00	2.00	—	—	2.00	1.30	1.65
Canada	1.80	1.80	2.00	2.00	0.80	2.00	0.30	1.50
Sweden	1.50	2.00	1.67	1.25	1.50	1.90	0.60	1.49
Philippines	2.00	2.00	1.80	2.00	2.00	2.00	1.35	1.44
Netherlands	0.67	2.00	2.00	2.00	-0.50	2.00	0.50	1.33
West Germany	2.00	2.00	2.00	2.00	0.75	1.60	0.20	1.18
France, 1959-1968	1.00	1.40	1.80	1.25	1.50	1.00	0.10	0.87
Yugoslavia	2.00	0.67	1.00	2.00	1.00	1.20	-0.10	0.85
Colombia, 1958-1967	2.00	1.80	1.60	2.00	0.00	0.50	-0.20	0.76
Italy	-0.88	1.67	1.00	2.00	-0.75	1.60	-1.10	-0.10
Means	1.46	1.76	1.53	1.87	0.83	1.61	0.45	1.29

a. See note 1, Table 16.
b. See note 2, Table 16.

1960, for example, President Garcia responded to allegations within his party and from the electorate about widespread graft in his administration by asking for courtesy resignations from the entire cabinet, heads of government corporations, and ranking diplomats. He then took this opportunity to reshuffle officials in a number of important posts. This is coded in our data as evidence of serious elite dissension.

Bitter factional struggles are common within parties and the administration, and their diverse and sometimes comic-opera character is not well represented in our scores. Late in 1961, for example, outgoing President Garcia made many last-minute appointments including the governor of the central bank. Garcia's successor, President Macapagal, then appointed another governor. Each refused to recognize the other's authority. The issue was resolved only when the second appointee persuaded the Secretary of Defense to order a constabulary company to occupy the central bank and evict the first.

Several coded cases of serious elite dissension occurred in the 1960s. In May 1962, for example, President Macapagal ousted two members of the opposition Nationalist Party from his cabinet in an effort to end bipartisanship. Other resignations, both in the cabinet and through all ranks of government, followed over corruption among high officials, brought to light by the Stonehill scandal. (Graft and corruption in Philippines politics seem scarcely less prevalent than numerous political and newspaper charges would indicate.) In 1964, a resolution to initiate impeachment proceedings against President Macapagal was defeated in the House Judiciary Committee by a 7-3 vote. In the election of 1965, following a bitter campaign that lasted almost a year, the Nationalist candidate, Senator Marcos, defeated Macapagal for the presidency. (Information from the *New York Times;* Corpuz, 1965; and a personal correspondence with Craig MacLean.)

The Netherlands, 1927-1936: budget efficacy: The government experienced no unusual procedural changes in formulating and passing the budget (done annually), even though financial policy proved to be testing ground for legislators in Holland, as it was for most European polities due to the economic exigencies of the time. Only after 1932 did crisis situations actually develop over finances, because of both dissension in government ranks and public protest centered on budgetary priorities.

In February 1933, the lower house rejected the government's recommended cuts for judicial and penal institutions. The Beerenbrouck Cabinet resigned, parliament was dissolved by royal decree, and new elections were called for April. Budgets in subsequent years continued to show large deficits. Protest riots occurred in 1934, precipitated by cuts in the dole and by high taxation. Pressures in 1935 to further reduce and balance the budget forced a showdown between pro- and anti-retrenchment advocates. Colijn resigned over the fiscal retrenchment issue under mounting opposition from Catholics and Laborites in July 1935, but reconstituted his Cabinet without a parliamentary majority at the end of the month. Reception of the Colijn budget in September was again markedly cool. In 1936, the economic crisis forced devaluation of the guilder and an end to the gold standard, bringing to an end the five-year struggle to hold the line.

Italy 1957-1966: allocation of authority: This decade saw many changes in incumbents, particularly at the highest level, although procedures generally remained constant. The government changed hands in virtually every year, usually when support was withdrawn from shaky coalitions or when confidence votes in the chamber were lost. The Christian Democratic Party dominated all cabinets in this decade. In 1962, a new political alignment of center-left parties was effected.

The Segni coalition fell in May 1957 after Vice Premier Saragat called upon the Social Democrats to resign. The successor Zoli government resigned in June 1957 after a recount of a chamber confidence vote revealed that the government was short unless Fascist support (unacceptable to several cabinet members) was included. Zoli, however, withdrew his resignation after attempts by others to form a new government failed. Zoli did resign in June 1958, following the general elections, to give Fanfani an opportunity to work out a coalition government, which Fanfani succeeded in doing with Christian Democratic and Social Democratic cooperation. By the end of the year, the Fanfani government, too, suffered because of repeated defeats of government bills in parliament. He resigned in January 1959 as the result of a split among the Social Democrats and of a general feeling throughout his ministry that his coalition of center parties was too unstable. Fanfani was replaced by Segni, who formed a cabinet comprising only Christian Democrats and not devoid of its own internal disputes.

Segni's government was defeated in February when the Liberal Party dropped its parliamentary support. The successor government under Tambroni resigned in April (after several ministers first quit the coalition), but was reconstituted. Tambroni's caretaker government could not deal with the crisis which occurred in the summer of 1960, however. It was rejected in both chambers of parliament because of its cooperation with the neo-Fascists, and was forced to resign on July 19. Liberals and Saragat Socialists (Social Democrats) offered the Christian Democrats their support in exchange for a coalition comprised of center and left parties, on the condition that the Christian Democrats reject the neo-Fascists. A new government with the parliamentary support of the Liberals, Social Democrats, and Republicans was approved July 26 under Fanfani's leadership.

In August 1961, moves were made to include the Nenni Socialists in the coalition. This new political alignment did not come into effect until

February 1962, however, when Fanfani stepped down to allow the formation of a center-left government. Fanfani headed the new coalition, which was dependent for its existence on Socialist parliamentary support, although the Socialists did not participate in the cabinet. This government resigned in May 1963, after the Christian Democrats suffered large losses at the national elections. Leone's brief caretaker government (Christian Democrats) was succeeded in December by a new coalition headed by Moro, following an agreement admitting the Nenni Socialists into the government. This cabinet comprised sixteen Christian Democrats, six Socialists, three Social Democrats, and one Republican: Socialists were again in government after an absence of sixteen years.

The years 1964-1965 proved critical for the coalition. The Socialists threatened to quit the cabinet in May 1964. In June, the government fell after a bill to increase state aid to church schools was defeated, but was reconstituted. The extreme right and left continued to undermine the position of the government, as did dissension within cabinet ranks. The resignation of Foreign Minister Fanfani in December 1965 necessitated a confidence vote, which the government won.

Comparisons by Country

We found that civil order and legitimacy increased in the polities of ten countries between the decades of 1927-1936 and 1957-1966. The same pattern is evident in decisional efficacy, when the budget and authority maintenance scores are weighted and combined as they are in Table 18. Average efficacy increased; the scores for most countries also increased, in some cases substantially. Somewhat surprisingly, the measured efficacy of all three continuing polities—Sweden, Canada, and the Netherlands—decreased. This may be an artifact of better sources for the second era, or more likely a real relationship. If the latter, there are at least two kinds of possible explanations: one that a political "hardening of the arteries" has set in which makes these older polities generally less efficacious, the other that the expanding scope of government functions intrinsically generates new sources of disssension and delay. We have no data now that might help us decide between these two alternatives.

The changes in efficacy across time are obviously not proportional among countries. Whereas the surviving polities declined in efficacy, six of the seven countries which experienced polity transformation between the first and second eras increased in decisional efficacy; the exception is Italy. Of those which increased, Colombia did so only slightly, as might be expected since the regime inaugurated in 1958 was a return to that of the first era. The others—Spain, France, Germany, and Yugoslavia—increased their efficacy by five to eight scale points, or, in relative terms, by two to three standard deviations. This close association between polity transformation and changes in decisional efficacy is unsurprising to those familiar with the political histories of the countries concerned; it does support the validity of the indicators developed here.

The cross-time correlations in Table 19 further quantify these generalizations. The correlations between two measures of budget efficacy, in the upper left quadrant of Table 19, show a low to moderate degree of continuity across time, scarcely a high one: the summary measures correlate only .45 with one another. The correlations among the measures of authority, in the lower right quadrant, are mostly negative and all insignificant: the summary relation between countries' efficacy in the maintenance of authority in 1927-1936 and their efficacy in 1957-1966 is precisely zero. Nor is there any relationship across time between budgetary efficacy and authority maintenance.

All-Polity Comparisons

Comparisons of the component indicators of efficacy for 21 polities are given in Tables 20 and 21. The budget indicators are satisfactorily related to one another, though procedural changes are relatively independent of timing

TABLE 18
SUMMARY EFFICACY SCORES CA. 1927-1936
AND CA. 1957-1966[a]

	1927-1936		1957-1966	
Very High Efficacy,	Sweden	4.97	Mexico	5.77
4.5+	Canada	4.66	Spain	5.13
			Sweden	4.66
Moderately High	Netherlands	4.48	Philippines	4.10
Efficacy, 3.5-4.4	Italy	4.16	Canada	3.72
			Netherlands	3.68
Medium Efficacy,	Mexico	3.35	Yugoslavia	3.07
2.0-3.4	Colombia	2.52	Colombia	3.02
			France	2.97
			West Germany	2.94
Low Efficacy,				
0.0-1.9			Italy	1.20
Very Low Efficacy,	Yugoslavia	-1.88		
<0.0	Germany	-2.38		
	France	-2.57		
	Spain	-2.79		
	Means	1.45		3.66
		Grand mean	2.61	
		Standard deviation	2.69	

a. The sum of budgetary efficacy (Tables 14, 15) plus twice the authority maintenance score (Tables 16, 17). The theoretical range of scores is +6 to —6.

TABLE 19
CROSS-TIME COMPARISONS OF SELECTED MEASURES OF DECISIONAL EFFICACY, n=10[a] 1957-1966

1927-1936	Budget Efficacy		Authority Maintenance		
	Dissension	Summary	Processes	Turnover[b]	Summary
Budget:					
Dissension	**34**	**33**	-14	07	12
Summary	48	**45**	-24	09	09
Authority:					
Processes	10	-04	**-31**	-16	-12
Turnover[b]	-03	-11	-37	**-02**	10
Summary	02	-10	-37	-09	**00**

a. Product-moment correlation coefficients x 100. None are significant at the .05 level.
b. Personnel change in governmental continuation.

and dissension. Among the seven indicators of authority maintenance, the stability of electoral procedures is only weakly related to the others. A glance at Tables 16 and 17 shows that electoral procedures are seldom varied, which further suggests that the indicator could be discarded in subsequent work. Elite dissension over elections also is only moderately related to other authority indicators, though not because of invariance. Elite splits tend to occur over electoral issues even in democratic polities that are generally efficacious. We also noted that in several otherwise efficient authoritarian polities—for example, both Mexican polities and Communist Yugoslavia—electoral systems were often revised and elections provided occasions for open intraelite conflict. The electoral dissension indicator will be retained pending the collection of data on additional, more representative polities; it may signify latent cleavages that are exacerbated under stress.

Finally, several summary indicators of efficacy are compared in Table 22. The r's are moderate to strong; budget efficacy varies somewhat independently of authority maintenance. The strong correlation of "authority processes" with the summary authority indicator and with most component indicators of authority maintenance in Table 21 (first row of r's), suggests that the "processes" indicator could be used alone in subsequent studies for gross comparisons of authority maintenance.

CROSS-POLITY COMPARISONS
OF PERFORMANCE

Two kinds of issues are considered in this concluding chapter: the extent to which our measures of performance are similarly high or low for the same polities, and their apparent causal relationships. Since our data are complete for only ten countries and 21 polities, verbal and graphic comparisons are as

TABLE 20

COMPARISONS OF MEASURES OF BUDGETARY EFFICACY, ALL POLITIES, n=21[a]

	Timing	Procedures	Dissension	Summary
Timing	100	27	56[c]	84[c]
Procedures		100	42[b]	47[b]
Dissension			100	86[c]

a. See note 7.

b. Significant at the .05 level.

c. Significant at the .01 level.

TABLE 21

COMPARISONS OF MEASURES OF AUTHORITY MAINTENANCE, ALL POLITIES, n=21

	Elections			Govt. Formation		Govt. Continuation		
	Processes	Procedures	Dissension	Procedures	Dissension	Procedures	Changes	Summary Score
Processes	100	05	40[a]	39[a]	63[b]	54[b]	76[b]	92[b]
Elections:								
Procedures		100	29	-07	03	32	40	25
Dissension			100	19	31	48[a]	38[a]	5[a]
Formation:								
Procedures				100	50[a]	50[a]	37	45[a]
Dissension					100	64[a]	76[b]	72[b]
Continuation:								
Procedures						100	77[a]	77[a]
Changes							100	91[b]

a. Significant at the .05 level.

b. Significant at the .01 level.

TABLE 22

COMPARISONS OF SUMMARY MEASURES OF EFFICACY, ALL POLITIES, n=21

	Budget Efficacy	Authority Processes	Authority Maintenance	All Efficacy[a]
Budget efficacy	100	59[b]	64[b]	80[b]
Authority processes		100	92[b]	90[b]
Authority maintenance			100	97[b]

a. From Table 18.

b. Significant at the .01 level.

useful as statistical ones, and conclusions based on statistical inferences are quite tenuous. The first subsection, below, summarizes some comparisons of the dimensions, the second deals with the causal question, and the last discusses the performance characteristics of specific polities and speculates about their future durability.

Dimensions of Performance

The durability of polities, we argued in the first major section, is largely a consequence of their capacity to maintain, over a long period, tolerably high degrees of civil order, legitimacy, and decisional efficacy. These three dimensions of performance all exhibit considerable short-term variation; longevity does not, or rather, as measured here it can increase only very gradually over time. To compare our summary indicators of performance other than durability, standard scores were computed from the pooled scores for both decades and are listed in Table 23. Their relations are graphed in Figures 2 and 3, for the two eras separately.

The increase in average performance between the first and second decades is substantial. By the standards of 1957-1966, a number of polities in the 1927-1936 era had unparalleled performance failures, notably the Spanish Republic, the Weimar Republic, the French Third Republic, and Yugoslavia's intial essay at constitutional monarchy. The profiles also make it possible to identify several different patterns of performance. The four polities just mentioned have more or less consistently low performance. Others, like Sweden I and II and Mexico II, have consistently high performance. A third pattern of inconsistent performance characterizes such polities as West Germany II, Canada II, and Colombia II: tolerably high performance on one or two dimensions is offset by low performance on others.

The summary indicators of performance are compared statistically in Table 24, for each era separately and for all polities combined. For the separate decades, polity durability is correlated in the predicted direction with the other performance measures in all but one instance: budget efficacy in 1957-1966 is not related to durability in the 1960s. Looking at the correlates of durability for 1927-1936, we see similarly that budget efficacy is the weakest of them, but appears to have a time-lagged effect on durability in the 1960s. Time-lagged relations are discussed further below. When all 21 polities are combined, in the bottom segment of Table 24, the pattern of correlation is entirely consistent with the theoretical predictions. Durability has similar, strong correlations with all the other performance dimensions, and most of the latter are significantly interrelated.

The inclusion of both authoritarian and democratic regimes in our sample makes possible another kind of comparison. Authoritarian regimes might be supposed to have more efficient decision-making processes than democracies,

TABLE 23
SUMMARY MEASURES OF PERFORMANCE IN
STANDARD SCORES[a]

	Civil Order[b]	Legitimacy[b]	Budget Efficacy	Authority Maintenance	Total
1927-36					
Sweden	0.52	0.78	1.20	0.67	3.17
Netherlands	0.49	0.94	0.12	0.84	2.39
Canada	0.68	0.61	0.18	0.89	2.36
Italy	0.68	-0.31	0.73	0.46	1.56
Colombia	-0.15	0.74	-0.17	0.02	0.49
Mexico	-2.47	0.11	0.15	0.29	-1.92
Yugoslavia, 1921-1929	-0.01	-1.24	-0.93	-1.77	-3.95
France	-0.57	-1.30	-2.66	-1.46	-5.99
Germany, 1923-1932	-0.36	-1.85	-2.37	-1.43	-6.01
Spain, 1932-1936	-2.86	-2.27	-0.20	-2.47	-7.80
Means	-0.41	-0.38	-0.40	-0.40	-1.57
1957-1966					
Mexico	0.31	0.94	1.10	1.08	3.43
Sweden	0.89	0.94	0.83	0.66	3.32
Netherlands	0.79	1.05	-0.01	0.51	2.34
Spain	0.47	-0.38	1.02	0.81	1.92
Philippines	0.12	0.94	0.24	0.61	1.91
Yugoslavia	0.84	0.49	0.43	0.06	1.82
W. Germany	0.71	0.91	-0.58	0.37	1.41
Canada	0.61	-0.02	-0.40	0.67	0.86
Colombia, 1958-1967	-0.59	-0.06	0.60	-0.03	-0.10
France, 1959-1968	-0.30	-0.14	0.26	0.08	-0.10
Italy	0.24	-0.86	0.47	-0.84	-0.99
Means	0.37	0.35	0.36	0.36	1.44

a. Standard scores computed using 21 polities as cases, for graphic comparisons only.

b. Signs are reversed so that highest scores are given to polities with lowest magnitudes of strife and illegitimacy.

as well as less strife. We categorized the 21 polities according to their regime type, combining authoritarian and quasi-authoritarian ones in a single category, and compared their average performance scores. The results are shown in Table 25. The most clear-cut advantage of the democratic polities is their durability (though note that the long-lived polities of Sweden, Canada, and the Netherlands are included twice in the sample). There is little difference in civil strife, while the authoritarian regimes appear on the average somewhat less legitimate. Their decisional efficacy is considerably greater than that of the democracies. The dubiety of these comparisons is the inclusion of a number of short-lived, very low-performing democratic polities. Their exclusion would substantially decrease the relative advantage of the authoritarian polities in efficacy.

Causal Relations Among Performance Dimensions

On substantive and theoretical grounds, we have speculated about the primary causal relations among the performance dimensions. These specu-

TABLE 24
COMPARISONS OF SUMMARY PERFORMANCE MEASURES WITH DURABILITY, BY DECADE AND FOR ALL POLITIES[a]

1927-1936	Civil Order[b]	Legitimacy[b]	Budget Efficacy	Authority Maintenance	Durability in Years 1930s	1960s
			1927-1936, n=10			
Civil order[b]	100	52	16	54	59[c]	20
Legitimacy[b]		100	65[c]	94[d]	75[d]	51
Budget			100	66[c]	32	63[c]
Authority				100	66[c]	57[c]
Durability 1930s					100	60[c]
1957-1966			1957-1966, n=11			
Civil order[b]	100	44	-20	32	05	67[c]
Legitimacy		100	-15	61[c]	23	37
Budget			100	15	45	-06
Authority				100	17	53[c]
All Polities			All Polities, n=21			
Civil order[b]	100	57[d]	24	59[d]	63[d]	
Legitimacy[b]		100	56[d]	88[d]	68[d]	
Budget			100	31	61[d]	
Authority				100	66[d]	

a. Product-moment r's x 100. Tunisia and the Philippines are excluded from the 1927-1936 comparisons because of their colonial status. Tunisia is excluded from the 1957-1966 comparisons because of missing data on performance.

b. Correlations for civil strife and illegitimacy with signs reversed to facilitate comparisons.

c. Significant at the .05 level.

d. Significant at the .01 level.

lations are diagrammed in Figure 4. To summarize the argument, we hypothesize that decisional efficacy has a primary and long-term effect on two of the other three dimensions: effective decision-making tends to enhance regime legitimacy and to reduce or eliminate occasions for violent dissidence. People's sense that a polity is "worthy," or legitimate, tends to inhibit violent attacks on it, and similarly to reduce the likelihood and seriousness of attempts to transform it. High levels of strife, especially conspiracy and internal war, directly threaten polity survival. Other causal sequences can be speculated about—for example, the possibility that durability and civil order ultimately enhance legitimacy. The causal model shown is probabilistic, one that we would expect to dominate in any large number of cases and over the long run. The model shown is not a closed one, since it does not take into account various exogenous variables that affect performance. Eckstein (1969) proposes that the congruence and consonance of authority patterns are major determinants of variation in all performance dimensions; the senior author has proposed that discontent and the balance of coercion are major determinants of magnitudes of strife (Gurr, 1970). Nonetheless, it is susceptible to several kinds of statistical assessment.

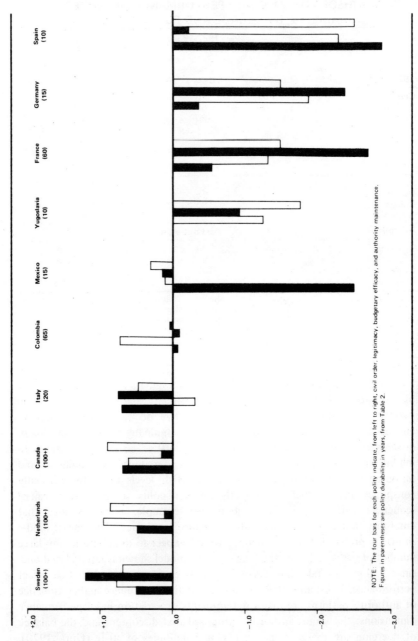

NOTE: The four bars for each polity indicate, from left to right, civil order, legitimacy, budgetary efficacy, and authority maintenance. Figures in parentheses are polity durability in years, from Table 2.

Figure 3: PROFILES OF POLITY PERFORMANCE CA. 1927-36

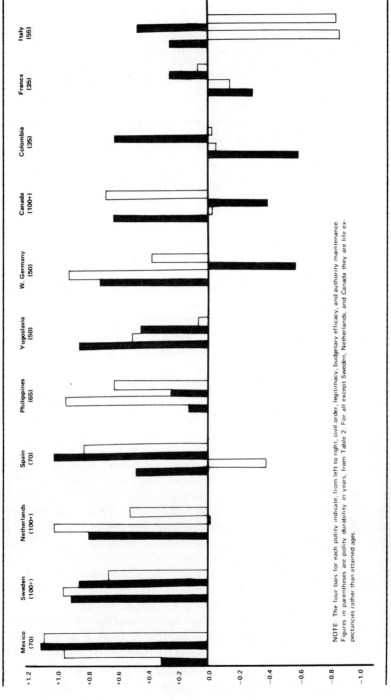

NOTE: The four bars for each polity indicate, from left to right, civil order, legitimacy, budgetary efficacy, and authority maintenance. Figures in parentheses are polity durability in years, from Table 2. For all except Sweden, Netherlands, and Canada they are life expectancies rather than attained ages.

Figure 4: PROFILES OF POLITY PERFORMANCE CA. 1957-66

TABLE 25
AVERAGE PERFORMANCE SCORES FOR DEMOCRATIC AND
AUTHORITARIAN POLITIES, ALL CASES, n=21

	Democratic Polities (15)	Authoritarian Polities (6)[a]	Difference in Standard Deviations[b]
Durability in years	64	43	+0.64
Civil strife	76	84	+0.10
Illegitimacy of regime	5.8	8.2	+0.37
Authority maintenance	0.61	1.26	-0.61
Budget efficacy	0.82	1.56	0.96

a. Mexico, both periods; Italy, first period; Colombia, Spain, and Yugoslavia, second period.

b. Difference in the averages divided by the standard deviation for all 21 cases; differences favoring democratic polities are indicated by +, those favoring authoritarian polities by —.

"Causality" may be manifest in time-lagged relationships among variables: X is said to cause Y if it regularly precedes Y. The decennial correlations in Table 24 are susceptible to this kind of interpretation, provided we make necessary hedges about the very small n's, the transformation of some polities but not others between the 1930s and 1960s, and so forth. *Civil order* appears to have the closest temporal relationship with durability: civil order I (in the first era) significantly affects durability I, but has little effect on durability II. Legitimacy I strongly affects durability I also and has a moderate time-lagged relation with durability II: its effects appear to be primarily short-term, secondarily long-term. Authority maintenance I has approximately equal effects on concurrent and long-term durability. Budget efficacy has only a time-lagged relationship with durability. The short-term relationships observed in the first era are approximately the same as those that hold for 1957-1966, though overall the r's in the latter are somewhat weaker. The time-lagged correlations thus are *consistent with* an argument that budgetary efficacy is the first or most remote determinant of durability, followed in a causal chain by authority maintenance, legitimacy, and finally civil order; they are not proof of it. We can also check whether durability has a feedback effect on the other performance dimensions by examining the r's between durability in the 1930s and the other dimensions in 1957-1966. These r's, which are blocked in the right middle part of Table 24, are all substantially lower than the reverse relationships between durability II and performance; no strong feedback effects of durability on other aspects of performance can be argued from these data. Quite the contrary: we noted in the major section just preceding this one that performance in the three most durable polities declined between the first and second eras.

Multiple regression offers a neater means of evaluating the time-dependent relations between durability, treated as a dependent variable, and the other three performance dimensions as independent variables. Table 26 summarizes the results of five multiple regressions. The first shows that efficacy, strife, and illegitimacy jointly explain two-thirds the variance ($R^2 = .66$) in polity durability during the first era; the second shows a weaker, time-lagged relationship between those dimensions and durability in the second era. The reverse relation between efficacy, strife, and illegitimacy in the second era and durability in the first is almost nil, $R^2 = .08$; this is, in effect, a test of the null or "feedback" hypothesis that durability substantially affects future legitimacy, strife, and efficacy. The multiple relation between the era II performance dimensions and durability II is moderate, $R^2 = .56$, and less than the .66 obtained in the first era. One reason statistical explanation is lower is that most of the durability scores for the second era are life expectancies, not true figures; the latter cannot be known until and unless polity transformation actually occurs.

Causal models of the type in Figure 3 also can be evaluated by examining the partial correlations among their variables (see Blalock, 1964; Alker, 1965). Generally, the degree to which one variable does or does not control the effects of another permits inferences about the direction of causality. If efficacy is mediated by civil strife and illegitimacy, then the partial r between efficacy and durability with the intervening variables controlled should approach zero. The partial r's in Table 27 support this prediction quite strongly. For all cases combined, strife and illegitimacy almost entirely control the impact of efficacy on durability: the simple r of .61 declines to .04. Strife has a moderate controlling effect; illegitimacy is much the stronger control, suggesting that it is more immediately dependent upon efficacy than is strife. (The effects are rather different in the two subsets of polities. In the first era, high efficacy seemingly *decreases* durability, when illegitimacy is controlled, while in the second there is no significant controlling effect. The n's are too small to put substantive interpretations on these subset differences.) The same patterns of control are evident when budgetary

TABLE 26
MULTIPLE REGRESSION ESTIMATES OF POLITY DURABILITY[a]

Period of Independent Variables	Dependent Variable[b]	No. of Cases	R^2	F Value
1927-1936	Durability I	10	.66	3.85
1927-1936	Durability II	10	.31	0.88
1957-1966	Durability I	10	.08	0.17
1957-1966	Durability II	11	.56	2.93
Both eras	All durability	21	.55	6.80[c]

a. Independent variables are magnitude of strife, magnitude of illegitimacy, and all efficacy. Although several of the R^2s are high, only one is statistically significant because of the small n's.

b. Durability measured in years.

c. Significant at the .01 level.

TABLE 27
PARTIAL CORRELATIONS AMONG PERFORMANCE VARIABLES

| | | Partial r's, Controlling for | | | |
	Simple r	Efficacy	Strife	Illegitimacy	Both
Comparison					
Efficacy I with Durability I[a]	.62	—	.48	-.31	-.32
Efficacy II with Durability II[a]	.45	—	.42	.33	.43
All Efficacy with Durability[b]	.61	—	.42	.08	.04
Components of Efficacy					
All Budget with All Durability[b]	.31	—	.20	-.11	-.08
All Authority with All Durability	.66	—	.46	.18	.11
All Strife with All Durability[b]	-.63	-.45	—	-.40	-.40
All Illegitimacy with All Durability	-.68	-.37	-.50	—	-.30

a. n=10.
b. n=21.

efficacy and authority maintenance are examined separately: illegitimacy very largely controls their effects on durability. Two other possible causal sequences evaluated in Table 27 are that strife and illegitimacy are indirect causes of durability, whose effects are mediated by efficacy. We see, in the last two sets of comparisons in the table, that efficacy and illegitimacy have a moderate, not a strong, controlling effect on the strife-durability nexus. Similarly, efficacy and strife partly control the illegitimacy-durability relation.

The results of the analysis on partials are most consistent with a causal sequence of the type shown in Figure 5, in which illegitimacy acts as an intervening variable between efficacy and strife. If the model is correct, we would further expect the partial correlation between efficacy and strife, controlling for illegitimacy, to approach zero. The simple r between efficacy and strife is −.53; with illegitimacy controlled, it is −.09, strong support for the proposed sequence. We emphasize again that the revised causal model is a probabilistic one, and based on a relatively small number of cases that are not wholly independent of one another. Moreover, it shows only the strongest links among the performance dimensions. There appears to be a moderate relation, of either a concurrent or a feedback variety, between illegitimacy and efficacy, and a weaker one whereby efficacy controls some of the effects of strife on durability. But these are, in this sample of polities, a good deal weaker than the dominant relations sketched in Figure 4.

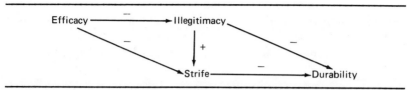

Figure 5: HYPOTHETICAL CAUSAL MODEL AMONG PERFORMANCE DIMENSIONS

An important implication of these results is that forecasting models of polity durability are feasible, based solely on performance variables. Let us summarize the results that point in this direction: we found that the time-lagged relationships among the performance variables, shown in Figure 4, are supported by both cross-lagged and static, causal-inference statistical comparison; and that multiple regression analyses yield relatively high levels of statistical explanation, in the .55-.66 range. These findings cannot be generalized because of the smallness and unrepresentativeness of our sample, though they do provide the basis for "forecasts" that we offer below about the longevity of some contemporary polities in the sample. But it should be possible, using performance data for a larger and representative sample of polities, to develop statistical models of this sort, which have at least a moderate, and empirically testable, forecasting capacity.

Performance in Specific Countries

The statistical comparisons give results that are consistent with our theoretical expectations but highly tentative in view of the very small number of cases. They do suggest interesting generalizations that can be applied to the discussion of specific polities and groups of polities included in the study.

The Stable Democracies

Sweden and the Netherlands are polities whose performance profiles (Figures 2 and 3) were consistently high in both decades. The Canadian polity also is conventionally regarded as a "stable democracy," although its legitimacy was subject to substantial challenge in the 1960s. The principal

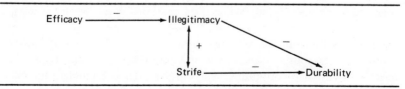

Figure 6: EMPIRICAL CAUSAL MODEL AMONG PERFORMANCE DIMENSIONS, SHOWING DOMINANT RELATIONSHIPS ONLY

evidence of performance decline among these three polities is decreasing budgetary efficacy in both the Netherlands and Canada, a reflection of both elite dissension and increasing delays in budget formulation. The same problem is apparent in West Germany, as it has been in the United States. There are two kinds of explanation of what seems to be a common phenomenon among the older democracies: budgetary inefficacy in Western democracies may signal the decreasing appropriateness of traditional budgeting processes to the increasing scope and complexity of governmental operations; or it may be that in well-institutionalized democracies, the budgetary process rather than authority allocation brings out the greatest elite dissension. If the former is the case, we would expect a long-term decline in budgetary efficacy in otherwise efficacious democracies correlated with increasing governmental scope; if the latter is the case, budgetary inefficacy would be expected to peak during periods of more general societal crisis. The latter explanation seems the more likely on the basis of the Dutch and Canadian experience during the two decades we studied: budgetary efficacy was lowest in crisis periods. The experience of the United States in the 1960s seems similar. But this kind of short-term cycle might also be superimposed on a long-term decline. Answers to these questions require longitudinal studies of more countries than are included here and over a longer period. Such studies also could answer better whether budgetary inefficacy, if protracted, leads to declining performance in other sectors. Unless we regard budgetary inefficacy as a bellwether of political disaster, our data all indicate strongly that the political system of the Netherlands will, like that of Sweden, endure without fundamental change for some time. Canada's survival is somewhat more problematic and could be better evaluated on the basis of its degree of success during the late 1960s and early 1970s in overcoming the separatist crisis and achieving substantial reform.

The New Democracies

The polities of the Philippines and postwar West Germany and Italy all are experiments in the establishment of viable democratic political systems in countries whose historical experience afford skepticism about democratic viability. The Philippines is a prototype of Western attempts to implant democratic institutions in non-Western political cultures. It has survived six years of autonomy (1936-1941) and 24 years of full independence without fundamental alteration of its polity, and it overcame a small but intense internal war, a better record than most other "new states." Its political culture also supports a great deal of kinship-based machine politics and favoritism, official corruption, and chronic political murder, unhealthy conditions for the body politic by Western European standards. Its performance characteristics as measured in this study are somewhat suspect for lack of detailed information, but they do suggest that the Philippines is archetypical of the general pattern, evident in some of our aggregate data, by which decisional efficacy can over the long run enhance legitimacy and civil order, and thereby create the conditions for long-term survival. During the 1920s and 1930s, the period of institutional transformation toward commonwealth status for the Philippines, the legitimacy of the colonially implanted institutions was low and strife widespread. The efficacy of those institutions was apparently high, however (according to data we have collected but not included in this analysis). There is no way of ascertaining to what extent the Japanese occupation contributed to a sense of national unity, but the data for the 1950s and 1960s indicate that strife has very substantially declined and that legitimacy has increased. Decisional efficacy is relatively high. Predictions about the durability of Philippine democracy are especially hazardous because no comparable non-Western democracies are included in our performance data, but by the comparative standard we do have, its middle-range survival prospects are good.

West Germany and Italy have parallel twentieth-century histories of ineffective democracy, authoritarian political solutions, military defeat, and democratic renaissance. The conditions of the renaissance were different, of course: the Germans were provided a product of their conquerors' constitutional engineering; the Italians themselves dispensed with their Fascists and monarch and devised their own new institutions. Perhaps paradoxically, the Germans have operated theirs considerably more efficiently. The success of West German democracy is seriously challenged only by budgetary inefficacy, which is almost solely a function of late budgets. If budgetary delay is regarded as an institutionalized or at least tolerable and not otherwise debilitating facet of the *Bundestag*'s existence, West German performance in 1957-1966 was comparable to that of the other stable Western democracies. The prognosis for its survival is similarly good.

Italy, by contrast, has relatively high levels of strife compared with other postwar democracies; its government's legitimacy is seriously challenged, principally on the left, but also on the right; and its efficacy in maintaining authority is lower than any of our cases except the four prewar European democracies which expired between 1929 and 1940. The high level of budgetary efficacy in contemporary Italy conceivably reflects elite consensus on national goals and allocation of national resources; more cynically, it may suggest that the elite is too much engaged in jockeying for power to worry about money. In fact, there does seem to be general, if not specific, consensus among the center political elite on the priorities of national economic development, which is reflected in high and sustained levels of economic growth and the lessening impoverishment of the South. The survival prospects of Italian democracy nonetheless seem much more problematic than those of

West Germany. More effective and enduring incorporation of the left into the decisional elite might increase the efficacy with which authority is maintained and probably would increase legitimacy and reduce some kinds of strife, hence, the chances of short-term survival. Political isolation of the left and the failure of economic policies is the kind of corrosive combination of circumstances that could lead to an end to Italian democracy as now practiced, and the imposition of authoritarian solutions of right or left. (We wrote these conclusions before the sequence of elite and popular crises that beset Italy from mid-1970 through early 1971.)

The Ineffective Democracies

Colombia, France, and Weimar Germany afford examples of seriously ineffective democracies whose inefficiencies contributed substantially to their failures. In both eras, Colombia has an inconsistent performance profile, and, moreover, one which worsens slightly between the 1930s and the 1950s. Strife, moderately high in the 1930s, was considerably greater thirty years later, though our summary data are somewhat misleading because the trend between 1958 and 1967 was a decline in the devastating rural insurgency and political feuding called *la Violencia*. Mixed performance in the 1920s and 1930s, and even more in the 1940s, undoubtedly contributed to the civil strife of 1948-1953, which led to the first dictatorship in seventy years of Colombian history. The failures of that dictatorship, 1954-1957, led in turn to another political renovation and a modified political formula. Apparent legitimacy declined from the first era to the second, principally because of popular hostility to and elite dissidence from the artificial and temporary political solution of "parity and alternation" in power established by the Liberal and Conservative Parties in 1958. One apparent consequence of the new political formula was an increase in budgetary efficacy, but conflict over the allocation of authority did not abate. The mediocre performance of the Colombian system under that formula does not offer a great deal of promise for its future durability.

The two French polities had the lowest average performance of countries studied in the two decades. Compared with the Third Republic, the Fifth Republic was characterized by greater legitimacy and improved decisional efficacy, but the improvement was relative only to past French performance, not to other polities. Moreover the Fifth Republic by most accounts came close to the brink of revolutionary change in May and June 1968, when it was scarcely a decade old. A qualification to this negative judgment is that the Third Republic did not succumb directly because of low performance in the 1920s and 1930s, but indirectly because of military defeat. Conceivably, it could have endured indefinitely. On the other hand, low performance was clearly a primary cause of military defeat, and also a source of the willingness of many Frenchmen to accept the Vichy regime. The French performance data point in contradictory directions for the future of the Fifth Republic. The secular trend is toward improving performance, hence greater longevity; the comparative standard suggests that the Fifth Republic will not be long-lived. French political history provides little warrant for optimistic predictions.

The data for Germany, 1923-1932, afford a cross-polity standard of comparison for the political disasters that have been chronicled in detail by historians of the decline of the Weimar Republic and the rise of Nazism. Performance was generally very low, notably on the crucial legitimacy and efficacy dimensions. Annual data, not reported in this study, make it possible to trace quantitatively a gradual increase in Weimar's capacity to maintain its authority up to 1929, followed by a precipitous and disastrous decline through 1932. The only less efficacious polity in our sample was the Spanish Republic.

From Inefficient Democracy to Effective Dictatorship

Spain and Yugoslavia both underwent essentially the same transformation between the two eras we have studied. After abortive and more or less disastrous experiments with multiparty democracy, authoritarian regimes were established in both and maintained relatively high levels of performance throughout the 1950s and 1960s.

Republican Spain was born in the ashes of an ineffective monarchy and died in a welter of blood. Its passage from birth to the beginnings of its death throes is included in our data. Comparisons of the pre- and post-1932 polities suggest that the republic's performance never improved on that of the monarchy and Primo Rivera's dictatorship that preceded it, but instead worsened. The inefficiencies of the succession of republican governments undermined the traces of legitimacy attendant on its birth and increased the polarization of Spain into hostile camps, with absolutely violent and disruptive effects. Low efficacy, illegitimacy, and chronic strife before 1936 did not in any deterministic sense indicate that civil war would result, but they did strongly indicate that the Republic would soon collapse under some stimulus or other.

The performance indicators of Spain in 1957-1966 offer a striking comparison. There was some strife, largely clandestine, and legitimacy was substantially lower than other performance variables, but both aspects of decisional efficacy were high. The comparative evidence suggests that efficacy is a necessary condition for long-term durability, and that it may also be a sufficient one. But of course the problems of the transfer of power from General Franco to the future king and the terms of power under his regime will be the proximate arbiters of authoritarian durability in Spain.

Yugoslavia provides another problematic case of imposed stability. The constitutional monarchy established in 1918-1921 was afflicted by continual, often violent separatism; its leaders were seldom long in office and almost never in agreement. An impatient monarch created a dictatorship in 1929 that nominally ended in 1931, and all the democratic frailties began to reappear. The Italian and German invasion ended a chameleon-like series of regime transformations, and, beginning in 1945, the one-party state under Marshall Tito provided at least a temporary set of solutions to the problems of low performance. By our measures, the immediate determinants of durability, civil order, and high legitimacy were strongly evident in the 1957-1966 decade; decisional efficacy was surprisingly low, only slightly above the mean of all cases. We found evidence of a relatively high degree of elite conflict over economic issues, as well as considerable party factionalization over the terms and allocation of authority, both present in unusual degree for a centralized authoritarian system. If the data and our interpretation of them are accurate, it suggests that the future durability of the regime is less certain that is commonly judged in the West. Despite the country's international stature and domestic economic success, and despite the regime's apparent popularity with its citizens, its elite may not yet have acquired the cohesiveness and capacity for cooperative decision-making that are requisites for surmounting crises and hence for long-term durability.

Effective Authoritarian Regimes

Fascist Italy and Mexico make strange categorical companions, since the first was a corporate state and the second was and is a nominal multiparty democracy. Despite formal and cultural differences both were postrevolutionary states whose modernizing elites worked through mass political organizations to create and maintain a relatively stable and essentially authoritarian political order in which open political competition was replaced by negotiations *in camera* under the guidance of a benevolent autocrat.

The relatively high performance of the Fascist state is apparent from Figure 2. It has less strife than any other polity of the depression era and moderately high decisional efficacy. Internal opposition was of course coercively suppressed, but even the Roman Catholic Church's opposition to the regime over a considerable period did not lead to any widespread popular manifestation of hostility or dissatisfaction. On the basis of the performance data there is little reason to think that the regime would not have long endured, aside from such imponderables as a succession crisis or military defeat.

Mexico during the 1920s and 1930s experienced a plague of crises, including violent elite breaks and several rebellions, that by all comparative odds ought to have led to the collapse of the polity. Instead, the outcome was a managed transformation. Between 1928 and 1936, a new political formula was hammered out: a new party, the National Revolutionary Party, was created and within it a balance of political power among competing interest groups was established and regularized. The presidency was linked to the party, later the Institutionalized Revolutionary Party, and thereby institutionalized, ending by 1936 the *caudillismo*-caused instability that had characterized the first two postrevolutionary decades. It can be seen from Figure 2 that even in decennial summary, the efficacy of authority maintenance was slightly above the comparative average. Some consequences of increasing decisional efficacy are apparent in Mexico's performance profile for 1957-1966: civil order was much greater, legitimacy enhanced, and decisional efficacy the highest of any of the polities in the study. Presumably there was much unreported dissension behind the scenes. Some strife is known to have been unreported, as is probably the case for most of our polities. But even the fact that more conflict was not reported from Mexico suggests something of the unity and efficiency with which the contemporary Mexican political elite has carried out the affairs of government.

A CONCLUDING COMMENT

Our judgment about the performance of these polities is limited. There are other aspects of performance about which data are needed and about which they can be collected. More detailed and more accurate information could and should be gotten on some of the dimensions included here, though they probably would not affect substantially the relative orderings of polities or principal conclusions. The information we have collected can be scaled and combined differently and analyzed in different ways, including the analysis of the annual scores, which we have not yet attempted. We are somewhat dubious about the significance of budgetary conflict for performance generally. Further analyses are more likely to qualify the conclusions drawn here than to suggest fundamentally different ones, however. Perhaps most important, the generalizability of the comparative findings requires data for many more countries and other time periods. We are continuing to collect and analyze information on performance, and we invite others to apply the techniques reported here to test the validity of our initial conclusions, and to answer other questions about political performance.

NOTES

1. Summary, decennial scores only are reported in this paper. Mimeographed tables listing annual scores for each country on each variable are available on request from the Workshop in Comparative Politics, Center of International Studies, Princeton University.

2. Former students conducting fieldwork related to our collective interest in authority patterns and performance were: Canada–Gurston Dacks and the late Peter Woodward; Colombia–Rafael Rivas; France–William Schonfeld; Germany–Ronald Rogowski; Italy–Alan Zuckerman; Mexico–Lois Wasserspring; The Netherlands–Philip Goldman; The Philippines–Craig MacLean; Spain–Joel Prager; Sweden–Robert Friedman; Tunisia–Donald Newman; Yugoslavia–Susan Woodward. Most of these individuals also reviewed the narrative materials on performance for these countries and made numerous helpful suggestions, though of course they bear no responsibility for any errors of fact or interpretation.

3. The life spans of polities in our two periods of reference, as shown in Table 2, were determined from more detailed information; they were not necessarily dated to or from the end of transition periods.

4. The 1958-1970 period in Colombia was transitional in the sense that an artificial parity of representation and predetermined alternation in executive office were maintained by the two major parties, with open electoral competition not fully restored until 1970. We date the current polity from 1958, partly because of substantial electoral competition during the period between shrinking "major" parties and their fissiparous offspring. On formal grounds, the new polity would be dated from 1970. Similarly, we date the French Fifth Republic from 1958 rather than from 1962, when the constitution was amended to provide for direct presidential election, on grounds that this was a constitutional capstone to de Gaulle's de facto dominance as president.

5. The skewness measure used is the sum of cubed standard scores divided by n. There is almost no skew in the distribution of the "years" measure. Note the polities of Sweden, Netherlands, and Canada are included twice in this comparison.

6. "Extreme bias" can result either from the deliberate nonreporting of strife, characteristic of some totalitarian societies, or from reliance on sources so summary that even strife of considerable magnitude is unreported, a characteristic of the *Annual Register*, for example, for many less-developed nations.

7. Three polities were excluded from this and subsequent all-polity statistical comparisons because of their colonial status, missing data, or both: Tunisia, both eras, and the Philippines, first era.

8. Summary scores were calculated by summing the Intensity and Pervasiveness scores and multiplying by Scope; see above.

REFERENCES

ALKER, H. R., Jr. (1965) Mathematics and Politics. New York: Macmillan.

ALMOND, G. A. and S. VERBA (1963) The Civic Culture: Political Attitudes and Democracy in Five Nations. Princeton: Princeton Univ. Press.

ANDREN, N. (1961) Modern Swedish Government. Stockholm: Almqvist & Wiksell.

BLALOCK, H. M., Jr. (1964) Causal Inferences in Nonexperimental Research. Chapel Hill, N.C.: Univ. of North Carolina Press.

BWY, D. (1968) "Political instability in Latin America: the preliminary test of a causal model." Latin American Research Rev. 3 (Spring): 17-66.

CORPUZ, O. D. (1965) The Philippines. Englewood Cliffs, N.J.: Prentice-Hall.

DIX, R. H. (1967) Colombia: The Political Dimensions of Change. New Haven: Yale Univ. Press.

DUFF, E. A. and J. F. McCAMANT (1968) "Measuring social and political requirements for system stability in Latin America." Amer. Pol. Sci. Rev. 62 (December): 1125-1143.

EASTON, D. (1965) A Framework for Political Analysis. Englewood Cliffs, N.J.: Prentice-Hall.

––– (1963) A Systems Analysis of Political Life. New York: John Wiley.

ECKSTEIN, H. (1971) The Evaluation of Political Performance: Problems and Dimensions. Beverly Hills, Calif.: Sage Professional Papers in Comparative Politics 01-017.

––– (1969) "Authority relations and governmental performance: a theoretical framework." Comparative Pol. Studies 2 (October).

ELDER, N. (1970) Government in Sweden. Oxford: Pergamon Press.

FEIERABEND, I. K. and R. L. FEIERABEND (1966) "Aggressive behaviors within polities, 1948-1962: a cross-national study." J. of Conflict Resolution 10 (September): 249.

––– and B. A. NESVOLD (1969) "Social change and political violence: cross-national patterns," ch. 18 in H. D. Graham and T. R. Gurr (eds.) Violence in America: Historical and Comparative Perspectives. Washington, D.C.: National Commission on the Causes and Prevention of Violence.

FLANIGAN, W. and E. FOGELMAN (1971) "Patterns of political development and democratization: a quantitative analysis," pp. 441-474 in J. V. Gillespie and B. A. Nesvold (eds.) Macro-Quantitative Analysis: Conflict, Development, and Democratization. Beverly Hills, Calif.: Sage Pubns.

GAMSON, W. A. (1968) Power and Discontent. Homewood, Ill.: Dorsey Press.

GURR, T. R. (1970) Why Men Rebel. Princeton: Princeton Univ. Press.

––– (1969) "A contemporary survey of civil strife," ch. 17 in H. D. Graham and T. R. Gurr (eds.) Violence in America: Historical and Comparative Perspectives. Washington, D.C.: ––– (1968) "A causal model of civil strife: a comparative analysis using new indices." Amer. Pol. Sci. Rev. 62 (December): 1104-1124.

––– with C. RUTTENBERG (1967) The Conditions of Civil Violence: First Tests of a Causal Model. Princeton: Center of International Studies, Princeton University, Research Monograph 28.

HUDSON, M. C. (1970) Conditions of Political Violence and Instability: a Preliminary Test of Three Hypotheses. Beverly Hills, Calif.: Sage Professional Papers in Comparative Politics 01-005.

LANE, R. E. (1962) Political Ideology: Why the American Common Man Believes What He Does. New York: Free Press.

LANGER, W. L. [comp. and ed.] (1968) An Encyclopedia of World History. Boston: Houghton Mifflin.

LIPSET, S. M. (1960) Political Man: The Social Bases of Politics. Garden City, N.Y.: Doubleday.

MERELMAN, R. M. (1966) "Learning and legitimacy." Amer. Pol. Sci. Rev. 60 (September): 548-561.

RUMMEL, R. J. (1965) "A field theory of social action with application to conflict within nations." Yearbook of the Society for General Systems Research 10: 183-204.

––– (1963) "Dimensions of conflict behavior within and between nations." General Systems Yearbook, 8: 1-50.

RUSSETT, B. M. (1964) "Inequality and instability: the relation of land tenure to politics." World Politics 16 (April): 442-454.

SOROKIN, P. A. (1937) Social and Cultural Dynamics, Vol. III: Fluctuations of Social Relationships, War and Revolutions. New York: American Book.

TANTER, R. (1966) "Dimensions of conflict behavior within and between nations, 1958-1960." J. of Conflict Resolution 10 (March): 41-64.

––– (1965) "Dimensions of conflict behavior within nations, 1955-60: turmoil and internal war." Peace Research Society Papers 3: 159-184.

TILLY, C. and J. RULE (1965) Measuring Political Upheaval. Princeton: Center of International Studies, Princeton University, Research Monograph 19.

TED ROBERT GURR is Associate Professor of Political Science at Northwestern University and Associate Director of the Workshop of Comparative Politics at Princeton University (1966-71). His general research interests are the applications of social theory and empirical techniques to the analysis of sociopolitical problems, currently including the comparative study of civil strife, social authority patterns, and governmental performance. Among his publications are a number of monographs and articles, and Why Men Rebel, *Princeton University Press (1970)–winner of the 1971 Woodrow Wilson Award of the American Political Science Association (for the best political science book published in 1970). He co-edited and contributed to* Violence in America: Historical and Comparative Perspectives, *a report to the National Commission on the Causes and Prevention of Violence (Bantam, Praeger, 1969). Dr. Gurr is a co-editor of the Sage Professional Papers in Comparative Politics.*

MURIEL McCLELLAND is presently a Research Associate at the Center of International Studies, Princeton University. She is the author of a technical report, Inequality in Industrial Authority *(1969). Her current research interest centers on authority patterns and sex roles in American society.*

A Better Way of Getting New Information

Research, survey and policy studies that say what needs to be said—
no more, no less.

The Sage Papers Program

Five regularly-issued original paperback series that bring, at an unusually
low cost, the timely writings and findings of the international scholarly
community. Since the material is updated on a continuing basis, each
series rapidly becomes a unique repository of vital information.

Authoritative, and frequently seminal, works that NEED to be available

- To scholars and practitioners
- In university and institutional libraries
- In departmental collections
- For classroom adoption

Sage Professional Papers

COMPARATIVE POLITICS SERIES
INTERNATIONAL STUDIES SERIES
ADMINISTRATIVE AND POLICY STUDIES SERIES
AMERICAN POLITICS SERIES

Sage Policy Papers

THE WASHINGTON PAPERS

SAGE PUBLICATIONS
The Publishers of Professional Social Science
Beverly Hills • London

Sage Professional Papers in

Comparative Politics

Editors: **Harry Eckstein,** *Princeton University,* **Ted Robert Gurr,** *Northwestern University,* and **Aristide R. Zolberg,** *University of Chicago.*

VOLUME 1 (1970)

01-001 **J.Z. Namenwirth & H. D. Lasswell,** The changing language of American values: a computer study of selected party platforms $2.50/£1.05

01-002 **K. Janda,** A conceptual framework for the comparative analysis of political parties $1.90/£.80

01-003 **K. Thompson,** Cross-national voting behavior research $1.50/£.60

01-004 **W. B. Quandt,** The comparative study of political elites $2.00/£.85

01-005 **M. C. Hudson,** Conditions of political violence and instability $1.90/£.80

01-006 **E. Ozbudun,** Party cohesion in western democracies $3.00/£1.30

01-007 **J. R. Nellis,** A model of developmental ideology in Africa $1.40/£.55

01-008 **A. Kornberg, et al.,** Semi-careers in political organizations $1.40/£.55

01-009 **F. I. Greenstein & S. Tarrow,** Political orientations of children $2.90/£1.25

01-010 **F. W. Riggs,** Administrative reform and political responsiveness: a theory of dynamic balance $1.50/£.60

01-011 **R. H. Donaldson & D. J. Waller,** Stasis and change in revolutionary elites: a comparative analysis of the 1956 Central Party Committees in China and the USSR $1.90/£.80

01-012 **R. A. Pride,** Origins of democracy: a cross-national study of mobilization, party systems and democratic stability $2.90/£1.25

VOLUME II (1971)

01-013 **S. Verba, et al.,** The modes of democratic participation $2.80/£1.20

01-014 **W. R. Schonfeld,** Youth and authority in France $2.80/£1.20

01-015 **S. J. Bodenheimer,** The ideology of developmentalism $2.40/£1.00

01-016 **L. Sigelman,** Modernization and the political system $2.50/£1.05

01-017 **H. Eckstein,** The evaluation of political performance: problems and dimensions $2.90/£1.25

01-018 **T. Gurr & M. McLelland,** Political performance: a twelve nation study $2.90/£1.25

01-019 **R. F. Moy,** A computer simulation of democratic political development $2.70/£1.15

01-020 **T. Nardin,** Violence and the state $2.70/£1.15

01-021 **W. Ilchman,** Comparative public administration and "conventional wisdom" $2.40/£1.00

01-022 **G. Bertsch,** Nation-building in Yugoslavia $2.25/£.95

01-023 **R. J. Willey,** Democracy in West German trade unions $2.40/£1.00

01-024 **R. Rogowski & L. Wasserspring,** Does political development exist? Corporatism in old and new societies $2.40/£1.00

VOLUME III (1972)

01-025 **W. T. Daly,** The revolutionary $2.10/£.90

01-026 **C. Stone,** Stratification and political change in Trinidad and Jamaica $2.10/£.90

01-027 **Z. Y. Gitelman,** The diffusion of political innovation: from Eastern Europe to the Soviet Union $2.50/£1.05

01-028 **D. P. Conradt,** The West German party system $2.40/£1.00

01-029 **J. R. Scarritt,** Political development and culture change theory [Africa] $2.50/£1.05

01-030 **M. D. Hayes,** Policy outputs in the Brazilian states $2.25/£.95

01-031 **B. Stallings,** Economic dependency in Africa and Latin America $2.50/£1.05

01-032 **J. T. Campos & J. F. McCamant,** Cleavage shift in Colombia: analysis of the 1970 elections $2.90/£1.25

01-033 **G. Field & J. Higley,** Elites in developed societies [Norway] $2.25/£.95

01-034 **J. S. Szyliowicz,** A political analysis of student activism [Turkey] $2.80/£1.20

01-035 **E. C. Hargrove,** Professional roles in society and government [England] $2.90/£1.25

01-036 **A. J. Sofranko & R. J. Bealer,** Unbalanced modernization and domestic instability $2.90/£1.25

VOLUME IV (1973)

01-037 **W. A. Cornelius,** Political learning among the migrant poor $2.90/£1.25

01-038 **J. W. White,** Political implications of cityward migration [Japan] $2.50/£1.05

01-039 **R. B. Stauffer,** Nation-building in a global economy: the role of the multi-national corporation $2.25/£.95

01-040 **A. Martin,** The politics of economic policy in the U.S. $2.50/£1.05

Forthcoming, summer/fall 1973

01-041 **M. B. Welfling,** Political Institutionalization [African party systems] $2.70*/£1.15

01-042 **B. Ames,** Rhetoric and reality in a militarized regime [Brazil] $2.40*/£1.00

01-043 **E. C. Browne,** Coalition theories $2.90*/£1.25

01-044 **M. Barrera,** Information and ideology: a study of Arturo Frondizi $2.40*/£1.00

*denotes tentative price

Papers 01-045 through 01-048 to be announced.

Sage Professional Papers

Editor: **Vincent Davis** *and* Mau

VOLUME I (1972)

02-001 **E. E. Azar, et al., Int**
events interaction an
$2.80/£1.20

02-002 **J. H. Sigler, et al., A**
events data analysis

02-003 **J. C. Burt, Decision**
the world population
$2.25/£.95

02-004 **J. A. Caporaso, Func**
regional integration

02-005 **E. R. Wittkopf, West**
aid allocations $2.5

02-006 **T. L. Brewer, Foreig**
tions: American elite
variations in threat, t
surprise $2.50/£1.0

02-007 **W. F. Weiker, Decent**
ernment in moderniz
[Turkish provinces]

02-008 **F. A. Beer, The polit**
of alliances: benefits,
institutions in NATO

02-009 **C. Mesa-Lago. The la**
employment, unemp
underemployment in
1970 $2.70/£1.15

02-010 **P. M. Burgess & R. W**
cators of internation
an assessment of ever
research $3.00/£1.

02-011 **W. Minter, Imperial**
external dependency
$2.70/£1.15

Sage Professional Papers

Administra

Editor: **H. George Fredericksc**

VOLUME I (1973)

03-001 **E. Ostrom, W. Baug**
R. Parks, G. Whitak
organization and th
police services $3.

03-002 **R. S. Ahlbrandt, Jr.**
protection services

03-003 **D. O. Porter with D**
T. W. Porter. The p
ing federal aid [loca
$3.00/£1.30

03-004 **J. P. Viteritti, Polic**
pluralism in New Yo
$2.70/£1.15

The 1973 summer/fall papers
03-005 **R. L. Schott, Profes**
service: characterist
tion of engineer fed